'Membering Austin Clarke

'Membering Austin Clarke

PAUL BARRETT, EDITOR

**WILFRID LAURIER
UNIVERSITY PRESS**

LAURIER
Inspiring Lives.

Wilfrid Laurier University Press acknowledges the support
of the Canada Council for the Arts for our publishing program.
We acknowledge the financial support of the Government of Canada.
This work was supported by the Research Support Fund.

Funded by the Government of Canada

Canada Council   Conseil des arts
for the Arts   du Canada

ONTARIO ARTS COUNCIL
CONSEIL DES ARTS DE L'ONTARIO
an Ontario government agency
un organisme du gouvernement de l'Ontario

Library and Archives Canada Cataloguing in Publication

Library and Archives Canada Cataloguing in Publication

Title: 'Membering Austin Clarke / Paul Barrett, editor.

Names: Barrett, Paul, [*date*], editor.

Description: Includes bibliographical references and index.

Identifiers: Canadiana (print) 20200300539 |
Canadiana (ebook) 20200301403 | ISBN 9781771124775
(softcover) | ISBN 9781771124782 (EPUB) | ISBN 9781771124799 (PDF)

Subjects: LCSH: Clarke, Austin, 1934-2016—Criticism and interpretation.

Classification: LCC PS8505.L38 Z755 2020 | DDC C813/.54—dc23

Cover images courtesy of the William Ready Division of Archives
and Research Collections, McMaster University Library.
Cover design by Guybrush Taylor.
Text design by Janette Thompson (Jansom).

© 2020 Wilfrid Laurier University Press
Waterloo, Ontario, Canada
www.wlupress.wlu.ca

Contents

Acknowledgements

This collection would have been impossible without the tireless work of the editors of *The Puritan* literary magazine. E. Martin Nolan and Tyler Willis were instrumental in transforming a scattered collection of ideas into the special issue dedicated to Austin Clarke's life and writing, which in turn became the basis for this book. I learned more about Canadian literary history, publishing, editing, and how to make a decent martini in the months we spent assembling that issue than at any other time in my life. Thanks, Ted, for your support for this project from the outset. Special praise, thanks, and acknowledgement is due to André Forget, who championed this project from the beginning. André is a sometimes-unsung hero of Canadian literature who has worked quietly, often behind the scenes, to support the work of Canadian writers in his role as general editor of *The Puritan* and in other capacities. I appreciated our rides to Hamilton to work in the Clarke archives and evenings spent visiting some of Clarke's own favourite haunts. André not only ensured that this book came into being but helped me understand Austin's writing in new, illuminating ways. André is a wise and insightful critic and the strengths of this collection, whatever they are, bear his mark.

Thank you to the archivists and support staff at the William Ready Archives at McMaster University. Your help in working through Clarke's archives, over a number of years, has been invaluable. Thank you also to my colleagues at Concordia University and the University of Guelph.

Thank you also to the collaborators and friends who generously provided their time and resources in supporting this project. This list is far from exhaustive but it includes Daniel Coleman, Patrick Crean, Dennis Lee, Loretta Clarke, Asha Varadharajan, Katherine McKittrick, Jean Marc Ah-Sen, Darcy Ballantyne, Rinaldo Walcott, Leslie Sanders, David Chariandy,

C.J. Bogle, Adrian and John Harewood, Judith Muster, J. Coplen Rose, Richard Cunningham, Sarah Roger, Guybrush Taylor, Emmy Anglin, Michael Bucknor, Neil ten Kortenaar, Ryan Perks, and Murray Tong. Thanks also to Siobhan McMenemy for her support of this project and valiant efforts to wrangle a particularly baggy monster into shape. Special thanks to Kate Siklosi for her endless support, friendship, and timely shade. Thanks also to Susan Keenan and Patrick Barrett for everything.

This collection is dedicated to the memory of Austin Clarke.

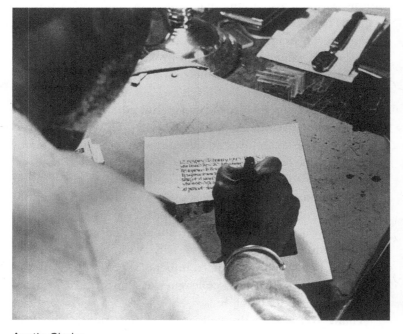

Austin Clarke.
Permissions: William Ready Division of Archives and Research Collections, McMaster University Library

CHAPTER 1

The Trouble of Intimacy

Rinaldo Walcott

Kinship is a wonderfully strange relation. Austin Clarke and I came to be kin. And, in the manner of most kinships, we shared an intimacy that I still struggle to make sense of. These works collected in *'Membering Austin Clarke* are striking for the intimacy the contributors share in their engagement with Clarke's writing and his life. Leslie Sanders's epistolary reflection on women in Clarke's work; Dennis Lee on their shared youth and editing Clarke; Sonnet L'Abbé on meeting him and his influence on and support of her; Katherine McKittrick on his library; John Harewood's exchange of personal letters with Clarke; Patrick Crean's experience as his long-time editor (*The Prime Minister* and *The Polished Hoe*) and close friend; and George Elliott Clarke on visiting Clarke's childhood neighbourhood in poetic form—all these evoke a certain kind of intimacy with Austin Clarke. And where the contributions verge on a more immediate intimacy, the readings and analyses of Clarke's novels, short fiction, and poetry all work at another level of intimacy within the fiction to reveal in detail the significance of Clarke's contributions, even when the representation he leaves us as readers troubles us. The mark of intimacy in this collection is, I think, very much conditioned by the fact that Clarke's own point of view as a writer was one of a carefully crafted and minutely documented observation of his surroundings. Clarke's fiction therefore always brings his readers into the intimate lives of his characters—from

Dots to Bernice to Boysie to Mary-Matilda to Idora, as any reading of his work makes immediately evident.

Intimacy is double-edged, though. I do not remember when I first met Austin Clarke. I do know that Dionne Brand introduced me to him sometime in the early 1990s and that we became fast friends. One of the sore points of our friendship was my significant lack in documenting my encounters and therefore my life. I do know that I had my first martini with Clarke (gin, the only way he felt a martini should be made) and I know that once becoming friends, we spent countless hours together in his home, in mine, and at bars and restaurants around Toronto. He loved sushi (California rolls in particular) and I was the one who introduced him to this cuisine. I still recall him exclaiming that his mother would be outraged he was eating raw fish. He grew dreadlocks when I challenged him to do so after seeing his uncombed hair (I, too, wore dreadlocks). For a period of about four to five years I rented and lived in the first-floor apartment of Clarke's house at 150 Shuter Street; prior to that he lived on St. Nicholas Street and I lived on St. Joseph Street. We grew to know each other well. He introduced me to his friends, his lovers, his acquaintances (of which there were many), and even to a distant relative of mine. (I would later find out that Clarke briefly lived with this relative and his family in Barbados. He was in his teens. I now take this story as somehow connected to the cosmic reason we became such good friends.) We were fully conscious of our friendship and often spoke about how a then-younger Black gay man (myself) and a mature, well-respected writer and public figure had forged such a friendship, even if our politics did not always align. We were often mistaken for father and son (he always insisted this was impossible because he was more handsome than me). Our kinship was a strangely pleasurable one. One thing was certain, though: we were both Fanonians and loved Black people.

The desire to vindicate a friend, a mentor, a father figure who has passed on is a strong one. I will continue to resist the impulse to do so with Clarke's work and his interlocutors. But let me pursue for a brief moment Clarke's relationship to women, both in his work and in his life, which was a deeply complicated one. Clarke, like most men, was a patriarch. It is not damning to make such a claim. His patriarchy was, if we could qualify the claim, of the soft kind. He loved women, he was afraid of women, especially his mother, and he was obviously conflicted by women in his writing and in his personal life.

If my argument about the intimacy of Clarke's writing holds, then, it is also a key to reading his female characters. Clarke's depiction of women was often an extension of women he knew in his own life. The fictional was never far from the real and I have met women who have successfully read themselves in his novels. Clarke did not dispute their readings and or the details of a particular scene and those women's memory of it as it actually occurred. Clarke's women characters are sometimes difficult to read because he attempts to offer us the details of lives that he observed, might have participated in, and as a way to come to terms with (his) masculinity. His work records how women are victimized and exalted and also demonstrates how he experienced women as both full of resourceful strength and as a force to reckon with. In many ways Clarke's fictional women are a composite of his mother and other women from his intimate life. I think we will have to seriously grapple with why women play such central and powerful roles in his fiction beyond their sometimes faulty representation. Thus, for me, it is not so much that Clarke is a misogynist as much as his writing spectacularizes misogyny in our culture. I do not offer this distinction as an apologia, but rather in an attempt to make some space for further insight into the man I came to intimately know.

If we read Clarke's writing of the city alongside his writing of women, the same mode or logic is at work. You can map Clarke's beloved Toronto through his writing. In Clarke's work Toronto is simultaneously intimate partner and vicious lover. From jazz clubs to street names to bars, Clarke's Toronto is one that invites and repels simultaneously. The short story "Canadian Experience" is at one end of Toronto, the end that repels, and in *More* Idora's

Kensington Market is at another end of Toronto, the inviting end. In the former the experience is driven toward suicide and in the latter Idora is lusciously enveloped in food, people, scents, and sounds. In both, the intimacy of life that I think underpins Clarke's writing is made evident. In Clarke's literary geography of Toronto, we are taken up in the intimacy of the city as a character fraught with all the problems, troubles, and double-edged affect that intimacy involves.

The archive of Clarke's life will never convey the intimacy that undergirded his passions. This anthology maps intimacy too through photography and Clarke's literary notes, his hand-writing and photos of his edits. The photographs offer some sense of what Clarke's life might have been like. Clarke curated those photographs much in the manner of his crafting of a work of fiction. Food, music, and good company were central to the environment that Clarke worked to create and those environ-ments also became the source for his writing. For example, when we hung out at the Sutton Place Hotel at Wellesley and Bay in the late 1990s, often for lunch, and found Coltrane playing, Clarke often claimed it was playing because they knew he was coming. Curation was central to his life—from cooking to dressing up or down to music to the carefully orchestrated invitation of guests to a meal or the selections of martini and wine for a party. And with Clarke, like any good artist, curation was also a kind of intimacy that could not be fully trusted either.

Since Austin Clarke joined the ancestors I have grappled with the double-edged nature of our intimate friendship and resisted the impulse to position myself as an arbiter of his legacy. Clarke is one of Canada's most important post–World War II writers and the first significant Black one. His contributions anticipated the multicultural present we now live in, and the detailed documentary process of his writing also leaves us documents of how we arrived where we are at in Canada today. In Canada, Black people and Blackness remains firmly adjacent to the national narrative that continues to imagine itself as white, a whiteness that Clarke's work spectacularizes for the violence it does to Black life. Clarke's writing career was touched by and informed by the brutality of Canada's white violence too. Given his contributions, one would think that he and his work would be a staple of what we now call CanLit in all of its manifestations and permutations. The story is otherwise. Indeed, some will seek to produce him as the grandfatherly incitement for their own institutional reach and as either a minor figure or a strawman that they must displace. Those attempts at minimization and displacement should be roundly refused. As Black studies becomes more institutionalized in Canadian universities, Clarke's contributions will be significant for understanding post–World War II Black life and white confrontations with Black emergence in that period. Clarke's life and work, therefore, demonstrates how in Canada Blackness and Black people are called on, discarded, and disremembered at will. This anthology, however, stands as a refutation of that ongoing problem for Black life in Canada.

Austin Clarke.
Permissions: William Ready Division of Archives and Research Collections, McMaster University Library

CHAPTER 2

On Austin Clarke's Style

Paul Barrett

Manners Maketh Man
—Gladys Clarke's mantra for her son
Austin throughout his life

Come to terms with me, I will not come to terms with you.
—Aimé Césaire, *Return to My Native Land*

When a writer leaves us, we are left only with fragments to draw upon, pore over, and reassess in an effort to hold onto some aspect of his being. In the wake of the writer's absence, words become talismanic, echoing a past made present and animating memories with the tenuous power of narrative. A manuscript's numerous editions, crossed-out sections, and marginal notes of self-doubt and admonishment bespeak the thankless hours and exhausting labour spent revising, rewriting, and reshaping a work. Letters of rejection and disappointment, intermingled with rare accolades and notes of acknowledgement, mark the milestones of a career built on perseverance. Unpublished works offer a glimpse of a writer struggling to be heard and to find a place in a literary landscape largely indifferent to his plight. We assemble these fragments in the hope of retaining the voice of the writer after his passing, of finding some solace in his loss, in conjuring his voice long after the writer has gone.

In the case of Austin Clarke, the fragments that comprise this collection give voice to his style as a writer, as a public intellectual, and as a man. We envision this collection as a tribute to Austin, a mapping of his work, a proclamation of the singular import of his writing, a refusal to leave his work unexamined and untroubled, and a measure of his contributions to Canadian literary culture. This collection includes scholarly critiques, personal reflections, biographical sketches, and poetic responses, along with interviews with and previously unpublished works from Clarke himself. The fragmentary form of this collection, speaking in various modes, across multiple genres, and with numerous lines of connection between the pieces, are themselves a tribute to Clarke's own fragmentary style.

This project began as a discussion between myself and three editors at *The Puritan* literary journal, André Forget, E. Martin Nolan, and Tyler Willis, on an April evening in Toronto in 2016. I had spent a few enjoyable, martini-laden evenings with Austin, and he was always gracious and generous with his time; we chatted about his writing, about history, politics, and life more generally. He insisted on buying the dinner and drinks for "the young professor" (I was a graduate student, but who was I to quibble). Inevitably, at the end of the night, when I crawled into a taxi, he explained that he would have a nightcap and then do some writing. I believed him.

Austin was, if nothing else, a man of style: he attended to his appearance with the same care and craft as his language. Every word was tailored and every paragraph measured against the cut of the larger work. His handwritten manuscripts are calligraphic works of art. Austin mastered the selfie before we had a term for it: his earliest author photograph shows him resplendent in a blazer, framed in cigarette smoke and his face frozen in a downcast, contemplative gaze. Later, he would match a grey pinstripe suit with circular, proto-Warby Parker glasses and silk kerchief. When he met the Queen, Austin combined stylishly coiffed dreadlocks with a blue suit and the tie of his alma mater, Harrison College. Style.

If ever the man or his prose appeared casual or easy, you simply weren't looking closely: sartorial, culinary, and literary style and splendour were equally important in Austin's world. As Katherine McKittrick's reflections on Austin's bookshelves reveal, the very space of his home reflected his authorial style of free association and hybrid form. Even his daily routine demanded a style: he typically woke late, spent the day reading and researching, ate nothing until dinner, had his dinner with martinis at the Grand Hotel, returned home and wrote until the sun came up. The poet and spoken word artist Clifton Joseph tells a story about Austin in which, after a night of drinking with some young writers and "retiring" two large bottles of rum, he poured Joseph into a taxi. As Clifton climbed into the cab, Austin said, "Now Clifton, a writer would go home and write." Clifton, barely able to stand, let alone write, said, "Write WHAT, Austin?!"

There was nothing simple about Austin's style: he treated a morning trip to Kensington Market—"the Jewish market" (*More* 194)—with the same sense of grandeur and occasion as a book launch or dinner with dignitaries. One did not simply shop for "ingreasements" in casual street clothes (196); such outings required a pressed suit, shined Bally shoes, an engraved pocket watch, and the day's *Globe and Mail* for the streetcar ride. As Asha Varadharajan notes in her interpretation of Clarke's work, "everybody has style," but some have more than others. Like his characters who drive Mercedes-Benz cars, smoke Gauloises cigarettes, drink Jamaican white rum, listen to Coltrane, and wear tailored suits and silk shirts, Clarke's style was a way of asserting a certain mode of masculine self-assurance. Possessing the proper objects and affects of style is a strong defence against Black invisibility in Canada or the regular accusation that Black men don't belong *here*.

Austin's attention to style was not merely masculine performance—although it was certainly that. Style, for Austin, was also a rebuke to Canada, particularly the Canadian cultural establishment, for its misunderstanding and misreading of who he was. Just as the establishment misread Austin, treating his skin colour as the key sign of his character, it also misread his work, misunderstanding it as a realist or sociological *account* of Black life in Canada. His writing has never been singularly realist, nor has it ever been reportage: it is a polyvocal, hybridizing, experimental, introspective, satirical, patriarchal, offensive, provocative, and—at times—outraged artistic *reflection* on life in Canada. His work, then, demands a stylistic account.

The opening of his final novel, *More* (2008), is exemplary of this hybrid, fragmentary, and transitive style. It begins with a description of the protagonist, Idora Morrison, as she awakens:

> Coming out of the dream, the bells are ringing, and she holds her breath, trying to find out the reason of the bells . . . she turns to lie on her back, and this makes her look up into the dark ceiling, and then all around her with the eye of a periscope . . . she is coming out of the reverie of the clutching embrace "that

Austin Clarke and Andrew Salkey posing atop a Mercedes-Benz.
Permissions: William Ready Division of Archives and Research Collections, McMaster University Library

man" has her in and the sounds of the bells of St. James's . . .
and in her mind she crosses Queen Street, then a small street,
Barton . . . then a bigger street, Richmond, then Adelaide, and
she walks through a small park . . . she enters the huge, studded,
brown stained main door of the Cathedral and, sits down . . .
and forgets her life, forgets her son, forgets "that man," forgets
the Island where she was born, and had left thirty years ago, as
an indentured servant, a "domestic" . . . for "the loneliness, the
loneliness, the loneliness," as she would complain to her friend
Josephine; and to her son, BJ . . . and now she hears the . . .
Cathedral bells, and tries to decide what time it is, but as she is
still lying on her stomach, she cannot tell if the three digits on
her alarm clock, 7.36, refer to nighttime or daytime. (1–4)

More's opening sentence spans four pages, evoking the memories,
dreams, ambitions, disappointments, and regrets that structure
Idora's life. The mobility of her stream of consciousness, jet-
ting from one faded memory to another, finds its parallel in her
fantasy of movement from her basement apartment (which is
actually Austin's own basement) to St. James's Cathedral (where
Austin is buried). At the end of the passage we learn that Idora
has not actually moved anywhere; her travels are a fantasy and she
remains sitting in the dark basement apartment, unable to tell if
it is night or day.

This passage contains many of the signatory elements of
Clarke's work: an intense working through of the past and the
narration of memory; the inescapable clutch of the demons of
history; a gesture toward emancipatory hope; a love of the language and ritual of Christianity; existential longing; the fear of
violence committed against young Black men; the desire to move
and reinvent oneself; and disappointment that often meets such
attempts at reinvention. These threads are sewn together as part
of a chain of equivalencies that grammatically and imaginatively
string together the bells, *that* man, her son, the space of Toronto,
the domestic immigration scheme, the coldness of Canada, the

cathedral, and, finally, Idora. The doubled nature of affect and emotion in Clarke's work is evinced in the mixed feeling of cloying entrapment and warmth in "that clutching embrace," in the possibility of a "breathless" awakening, and in the simple pleasure of a moment in which one is allowed to forget "the loneliness, the loneliness, the loneliness." This passage is exemplary in that it weaves together these dispersed and discontinuous fragments via the organizing logic of Idora's memories and fantasies—all that in the first sentence of the book!

Of course, an account of Austin's style would be completely inadequate without also attending to his misrepresentation of women. As Austin writes Idora for three hundred pages, keen human and social observation and his evocation of pathos at times veers into voyeurism, objectification, and fascination with a repressed queerness. Women in his work are too often objects of male style, projections of male fantasies: "the Canadian thing you see lying down there in that bed" ("Motor Car" 90) that match nicely with the leather interior of a newly purchased (or more likely, leased) convertible. Clarke's depiction of the women in his work regularly replicates this logic of possession, with characteristics pulled from a well of despondent female sadness from which Clarke never seems to tire of drawing.

As we saw in the previous chapter, Rinaldo Walcott views "Clarke's women characters" as "difficult to read because he attempts to offer us the details of lives that he observed, might have participated in, and as a way to both come to terms with (his) masculinity" as well as to demonstrate "how he experienced women as both full of resourceful strength and a force to reckon with." The difficulty of reading Clarke's women characters that Walcott discerns, both in terms of their intermittent complexity and outrageous objectification, is taken up by a number of critics throughout this collection. In her contribution, Leslie Sanders describes the difficulty of reading and teaching Clarke's work given "the increasingly invasive and visceral quality of your representation of women, particularly regarding how your female characters experience themselves. How to understand, communicate, and make meaning of their life in the fabric of your literary imagination?" Camille Isaacs's essay reads key moments in Clarke's oeuvre that show the recurring misogynist tropes in his later fiction. Sonnet L'Abbé gives us a sense of the man as patriarchal writer but also as a generous critic and sometimes mentor, while Asha Varadharajan offers an unexpected and spirited new interpretation of Austin's attention to sexuality and female bodies.

One of the central goals of this collection is to wrestle with these numerous *difficulties* and contradictions in Clarke's writing and to reflect on how a serious engagement with these complexities transforms our interpretation of his work and his place in Canadian writing. Indeed, it is a sad reflection on the state of Canadian literature that his work rarely receives such close critical attention. Were Clarke but a marginal writer, someone who made only a brief impression on our literature, this might be excusable. However, his foundational status in CanLit makes the lack of critical attention paid to his work all the more baffling. To take but one recent example, Nick Mount's much-praised *Arrival: The Story of CanLit* almost completely neglects Clarke's contributions to the Canadian literary scene of the 1960s. Mount's erasure is exemplary of a Canadian literary culture that has rarely understood Clarke's work. Take, for instance, *Quill and Quire*'s account of Clarke's Giller Prize win for *The Polished Hoe*.

> When Austin Clarke confounded the oddsmakers and walked away with the 2002 Giller Prize for *The Polished Hoe*, murmurs spread through Canada's tonier, gated literary communities that the wrong writer had taken the trophy this time out. *The Polished Hoe* was too long, they complained, its dense style too difficult and structureless, its tone too angry, too overtly political, too black. (Grainger 2008)

Clarke "confounded" the Canadian literary establishment. He didn't earn but rather "walked away with" the prize. Where previous criticisms of Clarke's work attack its apparent simplicity (see Michael Bucknor's chapter), here the work is thought to be "too difficult" and "too structureless." As Patrick Crean, Clarke's editor on *The Polished Hoe*, notes in his contribution to this volume, "When his name was announced, and they said 'The winner of the 2002 Giller Prize is Austin Clarke,' there was an audible intake of breath in the room and this undercurrent of 'Woah, how could this be?'" Charlotte Gray, writing in the *Ottawa Citizen*, echoed these sentiments when she expressed her disappointment that Carol Shields didn't take the prize that year:

> [A]t the Giller Dinner, I was Carol's guest at her table. When Austin Clarke was named the winner, I couldn't bear to turn around and look at her. When I finally did, I saw that Don Shields and Meg Shields were sitting close to her, one on each side, holding tight. And I also felt a huge wave of love and admiration surging across the room toward this fragile, blond woman. The three Giller judges may have chosen Austin Clarke that night, but Carol Shields had already won the hearts and minds of thousands of Canadian readers, including the Giller guests and particularly women. (2003)

Such observations are typical from the Canadian literati. Gray and Shields, Canadian critical insider and Canadian literary darling, respectively, are seated at the same table in an act of intimacy that bespeaks how CanLit is *supposed* to work. The too difficult, too political, too angry, *too Black* Austin Clarke is negatively compared to some "fragile, blond" people's darling; in other words, a *real* Canadian writer.

It demands repeating: Austin Clarke is one of our earliest, most widely published, best awarded, and least studied Canadian authors. His early stories and first novel predate Northrop Frye's articulation of "Where Is Here?" as a defining Canadian question. In the 1960s, at the outset of his career, he wrote columns for national newspapers, won literary awards, published in small magazines alongside Layton, Page, Cohen, and others, wrote for the CBC, enjoyed an international readership, and appeared on national television. Despite his contributions to Canadian writing and his status as a public figure, however, his work is absent from most Canadian literary history and criticism. Indeed, the worst drinking game in CanLit is to flip to the back of a literary history and take a drink for every "Clarke, Austin" entry in the index. You will be as sober as a late-career Leonard Cohen.

Clarke's writing and subsequent marginalization bespeak a rupture in Canadian literary discourse in terms of the voices it would include and the audiences it would serve. The rupture that Clarke's work represents is a precursor to the debates that have rocked Canadian literature in the past few years, particularly as CanLit's refusal to engage Clarke's work enables us to see how Canadian literary and critical communities imagine themselves and what difficulties or complexities they choose not to grapple with. André Forget's entry in this collection provides a sense of the cosmopolitan vision in Clarke's work that Canadian literature still struggles to recognize. Against a simplistic vision of a literature speaking for a nation, Clarke's work challenges not only the primacy of the nation as the lens through which we should read Canadian writing but also the voices, the styles, the languages in which the experience of this place will be narrated.

In the face of this ongoing critical neglect, the easiest thing for Austin to have done would have been to throw up his hands, accept that Canadian literature really means white Canadian literature, take a comfortable government job, and retire to his books, his jazz, and his martinis. But that was never his style. When we return to the fragments that inform our understanding of Austin as a man and an artist, we see that writing was what mattered to him most. The writer's life, the power of words, the capacity of language to crystallize a moment of transcendence, to capture the sting of racism or the dream of redemption—the ability of the writer to grasp at ineffable truths in fleeting moments that most of us only intuit—that meant everything to him. The word held such power for him: *writer.*

Clarke's style is therefore both a reflection of his own particular artistic vision as well as a response to the erasure and absence of spaces for Blackness in Canada. It is paradoxical and provocative for its eschewing of legible political categorization and for his strategic deployment of different styles calculated to provoke, anger, baffle, annoy, and entertain. When he arrived in Canada, white Canadians prejudged Clarke's level of education and intelligence. He thereby learned to use style to circumvent those presumptions and prejudices: his conversational and authorial style asserted his mastery of language, while his political style was an unexpected blend of Red Tory and Black nationalist politics. His wry acceptance, in the 1960s, of the role of "Canada's Angriest Black Man" and his subsequent transformation, in the 1970s, into a candidate for the Ontario Progressive Conservative Party, bespeak his strategies to both adapt and perform a style that demands a place for Blackness, in all its complexity, in Canada as well as to build a career for himself in a landscape hostile to his vision and his skin colour. His friend and fellow author David Chariandy details his difficult, "diagonal" relation to Austin both as a mentor and a friend.

Two of his editors featured in this collection, Patrick Crean and Dennis Lee, comment on the difficulty of working with Austin; that difficulty must be understood in the context of a literary culture that was suspicious of his very presence. Mordecai Richler, of course, believed he was wise to Clarke's game, claiming that Clarke used the myth of his own persecution in order to fuel his career (Richler knew this strategy well, having employed it himself).

Whatever his motivation, Clarke's style challenged, alarmed, confused, and intrigued; it could not be ignored. A great student of T.S. Eliot—whom he read voraciously at Harrison College in Barbados and emulated in his earliest poetry—Clarke's style owes something to the modernist master: repurposing the fragments of numerous voices, rhythms, histories, and traditions to be shored against his ruin, his neglect, his erasure.

I was standing at the corner of Hallam Street and Ossington Avenue on a Sunday morning when I learned Austin had died. It was three months into the planning of the issue of *The Puritan* that would eventually form the basis of this collection. The location is notable in his work, as it is the place where Albert Johnson, a Jamaican immigrant, was shot dead by the Toronto police in his home on a Sunday morning in 1978. Johnson's murder affected Clarke deeply: the figure of Albert Johnson haunts his characters' memories and nightmares throughout his writing. His prose is littered with visceral depictions of the smashed breakfast dishes, the imprint of the policeman's boot on the front door, the smell of gunpowder throughout the house, screaming children, and a man bleeding to death at the bottom of his stairs. If the iciness of the literary establishment was exemplary of Canada's polite racism, the police killing of Johnson was a horrific reminder that behind that politeness was the very real violence of white supremacy and the legacies of colonialism. Walking the laneway behind Johnson's home, I wondered whether Austin had walked the same space as he imagined how he might transform the Johnsons', and the Toronto Black community's, grief and outrage into some kind of bruised hope or balm against such violence.

Austin's style in response to the murder of Albert Johnson was that of mournful observer, enraged citizen-activist, and Jeremiah railing against the injustices of his society. He expressed his outrage in the Black community newspaper *Contrast*:

Anytime. Anytime I have to expect. that a policeman. who dislikes my love of flowers. who feels that I am man. can kick in my door: overturn my Sunday pot of rice and peas: beat me while I am on bended knee. and then kill me. He can kill me in the presence of my children and my wife. He can do all those things to me. because he has the power. and the authority. Because he has determined. on his own. that I am his enemy. And also because he feels that his conduct. his indecency may not be chastisably reprehensible by his colleagues and his superiors. (12)

Clarke's anger is palpable: the staccato sentences bespeak the cut of the police bullets, the naked violence of the killing. Language fails in the face of such terror, which reminds Black men that, even in their homes, they aren't safe from the police. Yet as the editorial continues, Clarke recovers his usual loquacious tone. Here style becomes both a weapon and a mirror held up to Canadian society in order to unmask the "indecency" of the law and of white Canada's indifference to Black life.

This indifference, and outright violence, continues today, and it is one of the reasons we continued pursuing this project after Austin's death. Our first intuition was that we might abandon the collection altogether, particularly as it took on a new gravitas. Austin's story was not necessarily ours to tell, and perhaps some more appropriate venue or publication—a publisher that Austin had worked with in the past—would be preparing a similar reflection on his work. But as his death received minimal attention in the Canadian press, and as his work continued to suffer critical neglect, this collection seemed ever the more necessary. Indeed, the anniversaries of Austin's death have passed with little notice in either Canadian literary circles or public forums. His books are largely out of print; his house, an archive of Canadian literary history and a central node in the cultural life of Toronto, remains derelict and untouched. More importantly, however, the words of encouragement we received from Austin's friends and colleagues—many of whom are included in this volume—confirmed that this project should go ahead. That so many of Austin's admirers, critics, colleagues, and friends have contributed excellent pieces to this collection perhaps indicates that we were right to continue with the project. Besides, quitting wasn't Austin's style.

I became familiar with Austin's spirit of persistence from my time spent working in his archives at McMaster University; I first visited as a graduate student when I was writing a history of *More*. It took Austin thirty years to write the novel, and it underwent at least twelve substantial transformations. In the late 1970s, he bragged to his friend Sam Selvon that he was "dreaming of the millions" that were to arrive with the imminent publication of the novel; it finally came out in 2009.

Austin's archives are a lesson in indefatigable persistence. They are filled with unpublished manuscripts, rejection letters, ideas for TV shows and plays, short stories and interviews, most of which have never seen the light of day. His archives are a catalogue of some successes, but mostly of failures—a monument to the experience of failing, again and again, and never wavering in the belief in one's own talent, until that rare, unlikely moment when something sticks.

That time in the archive was revelatory for me—I spent those humid, pleasurable summer days in the silence of a library basement, steeped in the drama of events that occurred before I was alive. It quickly became clear to me that the published text was just one of the many pieces that together comprise the author's story: the numerous drafts of novels, the midnight notes, the newspaper clippings, the BMW receipts (really), the letters of abuse from Austin to his editors, Austin to his friends, Austin to his enemies—these fragments all shape how we read the work and how we come to know the man.

Working in the archive also gave me a sense of the material necessity of Austin's fragmented style: he recycled and repurposed his own work whenever he could. Early drafts of novels are retitled, cut down into short stories, passed off as new work, and sold to a willing bidder. Whole swaths of unpublished manuscripts make appearances in subsequent works, awkwardly jammed into a narrative frame in which they hardly fit. A short story can become a radio play, can become a theatre production, can be become the basis for an editorial, can become a novel. In this respect his style is in some ways that of the rag-and-bone author: no part need be discarded, it can always be repurposed for some other project.

Indeed, the archive itself is a lesson in repurposing one's artistic work in order to survive. Austin strategically donated his archives in the years that align with the release of his major publications so that the tax receipt for his donation would be most lucrative. In this respect the archive itself is a dimension of Austin's style, what Idora calls "Survival, girl! Improvisation" (*More* 58). Austin improvises, transforming letters from creditors

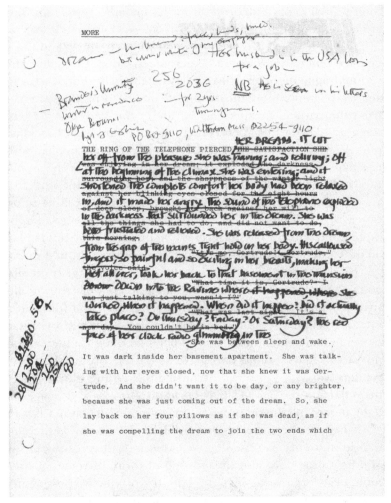

Austin Clarke's revisions of the opening of *More*.

Permissions: William Ready Division of Archives and Research Collections, McMaster University Library

demanding overdue payments into new material for the archives and therefore turning debt into another source of income. There is something very Austin about reading a letter, in the archive, complaining that McMaster are a bunch of cheap bastards for their refusal to pay him properly for his material. Style: improvisation, survival, performance.

Austin had a range of styles upon which to draw, and these enabled him to improvise in his acts of narration. Compiling the various fragments of his style reveals what might be described as an aggressive creolization: the mixing of cultural forms that emerges from the particular experience of life in the Caribbean. There are a number of links between creolization and what Canadian poet A.J.M. Smith calls "eclectic detachment:" the Canadian writer's experience of being "immersed both in the European and the North American cultural tradition . . . but . . . not of it" (8). Yet detachment and creolization aren't quite right. Clarke could never be as disengaged as Smith's modernist poet. Similarly, despite the sense of blending, creolization retains the fundamental differences and integrity between the distinct cultural forms.

Clarke goes further than detachment, borrowing, or creolization to practise what I think of as an aesthetics of crossing: his style crosses a range of cultural, aesthetic, historical forms in a way that renders them forever contaminated; he destroys whatever safe limits might have existed between those traditions. It is not merely that he shows Caribbean people in Toronto—his work renders Toronto Caribbean. Winfried Siemerling intuits this in his reflection on Clarke's play on musical tropes and images of light, describing the "improvised transposition" at play in Clarke's work. Indeed, the title of his first novel, *The Survivors of the Crossing*, indicates not just the crossing of diaspora or the crossing of the Middle Passage but also his crossing of form, of voice, of tradition, of style. Crossing includes both the productive possibilities of hybridity and bricolage as well as the misrecognition and violence that inevitably occur when cultures meet.

Describing the experience of reading Chaucer in colonial Barbados, he writes, in his second memoir, *'Membering*, "as my mother said, 'one thing led to another'; and we used Chaucer's language of the fourteenth century to daub the personality and character of our colleagues sitting beside us. . . . We went through the list of pilgrims, from the General Prologue, and transferred them, to our colleagues" (247).

"One thing led to another." Like Idora's chain of equivalencies linking memory, history, desire, and hope, Clarke's experience in the Bajan classroom adapts Chaucer's pilgrims to fit these young colonial subjects. The "stupidness" of Clarke's education was that it better prepared him to be an ideal, obedient colonial subject than to face the challenges of modern Barbados. In the face of such stupidness, Clarke adapted, using style to transform an imported set of narrative forms and tools to fit his circumstances.

An exemplary instance of Clarke's fragmentary style of crossing is found in his tribute to his friend and fellow novelist Sam Selvon in *A Passage Back Home*. Writing after Selvon's passing, Clarke recalls the first time he heard his friend's work being read on the BBC program *Caribbean Voices*:

> I cannot remember what time it was, when I first heard, either his voice or the magnificent acquainted language of his stories, sent back to us from overseas; . . . our words spoken amongst us, in fragments and with no force of appeal, would be golden portraits of our lives, because they were coming to us on these Sunday nights, from overseas: on the BBC's radio programme, "Caribbean Voices". . . . [T]o hear, all of a sudden about the breadfruit tree; the casaurinas; the names of flowers we had passed earlier that very Sunday . . . the Kiskides, Couva, Port of Spain, Gravesend Beach and "Trumper": to hear these symbols of words, greater than words; greater than our recognition of them in everyday life, all this was to make us feel "we was people, too." (9–12)

The language of the Caribbean is transformed as it flies across the Atlantic, recast in the medium of radio and blended with the voice of the BBC in order to be made new. Clarke's own "magnificent acquainted language" is broken apart into "fragments" only to be reassembled, through the act of narration, as "golden portraits of our lives." The familiar vocabulary of "breadfruit tree," "casaurinas," "Kiskides," "Couva," "Trumper" is given a new vitality precisely as it becomes defamiliarized and fragmented. Like Idora, lying in her bed in the basement apartment in Moss Park, imagining movement across a city that otherwise ignores her, young Clarke sits in his home in Barbados next to the radio, allowing Selvon's words to transport him across the Atlantic, and then back "home," only to find home beautifully disfigured and depicted in a new, golden light. At the heart of Clarke's style, therefore, is the capacity to cross these fragments of memory, history, desire, and longing in the articulation of some new imagined self.

Clarke's fragments, as well as his attention to the act of sewing those fragments together, crossing them in new ways—these insist upon writing itself as the primary scene of his style. Perhaps the theme to which Clarke returns most regularly throughout his oeuvre is that of writing. Writing is the space where the fragments are crossed together not to form some cohesive or sutured whole but to revel in the act of telling in order to know one's ironies, to celebrate the power and joy of words, to find brutal and honest truths in the act of narrating oneself. It is little surprise, then, that Clarke's first novel, *The Survivors of the Crossing*, begins with the protagonist, Rufus, working on a sugar cane plantation and palming a letter from a friend in Canada. The letter sets everything in motion. Writing, and the act of narration, is perhaps *the* way in which Clarke's characters string together the fragments of their existences, the confusing pressures of migration, and the disappointments of life. Rufus imagines a "feeling of pride gathered deep in his heart: to think that he was the recipient of this important-looking airmail from overseas! From a large continent, sent to him on this small island! . . . From so many miles across the seas, and [it] had landed right here, in the correct place, in the correct Village!" (4).

The arrival of the letter, which Rufus cannot read, reshapes his imagination. He goes from feeling he exists on the absolute margins of the British Empire to imagining himself as part of an international network of exchange of ideas. Of course, things don't turn out as Rufus hoped, but the arrival of the letter nonetheless initiates a chain of events that transforms Rufus's relationship to the space of the plantation. While Rufus cannot read the letter, he knows the power of words; when he hears it read aloud he senses "something basic and vital . . . [to] have that power o' words and ideas in his hand. . . . It read like a piece o' poetry" (11). Similarly, in *Amongst Thistles and Thorns*, Girlie feels like "I got the first prize!" when she is the recipient of "a first-class, registered air mail red-white-and-blue envelope . . . with a picture of Abraham Lincoln, the man who freed the slaves" containing "a real ten-dollar bill, made in the United States of America, with 'In God We Trust' printed on it" (65). It is not merely the words themselves, but the idea of language—words as a metonym for freedom and possibility. In his final collection of poetry, *In Your Crib*, the speaker laments that "I do not have the gift of words / put down in certain rhyme and rhythm / to guide your hand" (45). It is little surprise, then, that the original title of *Survivors* was "Words, Words, Words, is the Future."

The plot of Clarke's best-known novel, *The Polished Hoe*, constitutes a lengthy confession wherein Mary-Mathilda tells Sergeant Percy the story of the plantation and her murder of the plantation owner. The confession lasts a whole night and Mary-Mathilda expands her confession into a narration of the history of slavery, colonialism, migration, and the experience of Black people in Barbados. Her confession weaves together these fragments and, as she explains to Percy, "all that we possess to hand-down is love. And bitterness. And blood. And anger. And all four, wrap-up in one narrative" (354).

Mary-Mathilda's summative words give perhaps the finest encapsulation of Clarke's style: an effort to wrap the fragments of experience into one cohesive narrative, in a manner that makes the act of writing, the love of language, and the very human drive to tell a story the organizing thread that weaves together human disorder and the messiness of life into something we can recognize and see ourselves in. Clarke's prose simultaneously attends to the style of the self and the style of the letter, making writing and language the scene of self-making. His characters are always writing letters, telling stories, confessing their acts, retreading the ground of their lives. All in the hope of some new insight, some possible resolution, some respite from struggle, or a moment of grace in the act of retelling. To be a *writer* is to be seen, to be heard. *This* is the ultimate act of style for Clarke.

CHAPTER 3

Dear Austin: Why Teaching Your Work Is Difficult

Leslie Sanders

Dear Austin,

I've been reading your work for many years, and known you since the 1970s, in fact, and think I do truly understand and appreciate your importance. I no longer recall how we met, except that it was before I won a post-doctoral fellowship to write about your work; we did speak, then, several times, and I remember that you were very pleased with the essay I produced as a result. You lived a block away in those years, and would invite me around from time to time; I recall one long visit on Bloom's Day listening to a reading of the entirety of James Joyce's *Ulysses*. Later, many others— with mutual friends, especially Rinaldo, dear to both of us— spent evenings at your home or his, or your various haunts, just hanging out, over the years. Doctor or Professor, you always called me; not a close friendship, but a long one, one based, I think, on mutual respect and fondness. As you know, I teach African-Canadian literature on both the undergraduate and graduate level, and every time I put together a syllabus, I am torn as regards your work and what to assign. Especially at the undergraduate level. What can I teach of your work that will not make me feel I must attack, defend, or ignore your representation of women? And if attack is my only viable option, how will that affect how succeeding generations value your work and contributions?

Of course, you are not alone by any means in regard to this problem, and many factors contribute to the narrowly gendered perspective of your imaginative world. At root, I think your project, of historical and continued importance, is the making of men, the difficulties of manhood in the aftermath of slavery, colonialism, Caribbean independence, and migration to white majority metropolises (in your case, Toronto)—even when women are central to your narrative. Your early work focuses on women in part because, due to the Domestic Scheme, they came first, providing a means and gateway for male arrival. Later, well, perhaps what follows will suggest what I see as the complexities of your later major characters: Mary-Mathilda and Idora.

Of major importance, your fiction introduced Caribbean people to Toronto, and the converse, chronicling migrant lives in narratives unabashedly flooded with a Barbadian-infused vernacular, and insistent upon the migrants' perspective on Canadian life, its limitations, its racism—and in their own tongue. Your work began at the renaissance of Canadian literature, and for many years was its major, virtually singular Black voice in major Canadian publishers and presses. Speaking for community, and to an essentially hostile other, while still critiquing both, is part of the genius of your accomplishment.

There is a lot one can say, academically speaking, about the hows and whys and whats regarding your representations. It is not my intention here to pursue that avenue. I take this informal approach to allow myself speculation perhaps not permissible in traditional scholarly form, and to wrestle with what I experience as the increasingly invasive and visceral quality of your representation of women, particularly regarding how your female characters experience themselves. How to understand, communicate, and make meaning of their life in the fabric of your literary imagination?

Women are central to much of your early writing. In the Toronto Trilogy, for example, it is Bernice and then Estelle who carry the narrative in the first two volumes, and with whose fate we are most concerned, and while Boysie is the central conscious-ness in the third volume, Dots is made vivid in her loneliness. I've long regarded one story in your early collection *When He Was Free and Young and He Used to Wear Silks*, "Waiting for the Postman to Knock," as a touchstone for thinking about your early representa-tion of women. So abject is Enid's situation in that story, so devoid of hope, that her weeping and her rage seem barely adequate a response to her situation. Everyone wants something from her: her mother and her boyfriend, the landlord, Bell and Hydro, and she has nothing. At the story's conclusion, Christmas Eve, she sits alone in the dark. ". . . Enid didn't know nothing about time now, and she didn't really know where she was; here or there . . . she sit down on the toilet bowl to pass water, and as she sit there she cry and cry and cry out . . ." (50). The depth of disappointment, sorrow, betrayal, and despair contained in these pages could only be expressed by a woman in your fictional universe. It is not that your male characters do not feel similarly, but they have no means of expressing it, no means but madness and suicide. I've long thought that vulnerabil-ity enters your fiction through your Black women characters.

Strikingly, in your preface to *Nine Men Who Laughed*, you situ-ate your vexed and hurtful relationship with Canada as with a rejecting white woman ("the *person* who confronted me with her prepossessiveness, the woman, the system [sic]" [3]), and many of your stories concern relationships between Black men and white women, virtually all of which are based on manipulation and deception. However, that theme subsides after your novel *The Question*, which seems fully to explore and excavate that kind of relationship (or that is my reading), with its plot of a marriage between a Black man and a white woman vexed by her fixation on her little dog, and finally abandoned by the male character when he discovers her sexual relationship with her female best friend.

More generally, in your fiction, your male characters express a vivid and casual sexism, their relationship with women an expres-sion of their gendered right and prowess. You construct some powerful and arresting female characters, notably, of course, in *The Polished Hoe*, but you write no love stories, no relationships based on, nor stories depicting, mutuality.

The persistent and conventional sexism and misogyny in your work is difficult and problematic; however, more recently, your representation of women occasionally has taken a turn that might simply be experienced as a kind of pornography; for example, in "Our Lady of the Hours," where a woman masturbates while talking to her friend on the phone. To me, however, upon reflection, such scenes also have a deeper resonance. A few years ago, while reading *More*, your last novel, with a graduate class, a student commented about your representation of Idora's highly physical self-engagement during her retreat: "Give the woman her privacy!" The comment was very apt. *More* opens on Idora's dream in which ringing church bells transform into a man's touch, bringing her to orgasm; later she sashays around her tiny basement apartment vamping for the mirror and touching herself seductively. In comparison to other narratives centred on women, including *The Polished Hoe*, the narrative voice wishes to inhabit Idora, to become her. The gaze so frequent in your other work has become internalized, self-reflexive. There is a path from Enid to Idora, I think, ultimately a desire not only to write the woman but to inhabit her, not only her mind but her body as well. A kind of cross-dressing, if you will. It's not an idea I had expected when thinking about this letter to you, and I wish you were able to respond. Actually, I don't imagine you would recoil.

The problem remains for me, but also the urgency of your work, as relevant as it was when you began writing, both for that institution called Canadian literature and as narrator of Black Diaspora story.

So, perhaps others will have suggestions. I'm still at a loss.

Your friend,
Leslie

"There Were No Elders. Only Old Men": Aging and Misogyny in Austin Clarke's Later Fiction

Camille Isaacs

In a recent article in *The Guardian* newspaper, writer Jonathan McAloon asks if male writers can avoid misogyny. The central question he poses is, "how does one write about misogyny without perpetuating it?" (2017). It is a question that has been shadowing Austin Clarke's work for decades. In 1994, Stella Algoo-Baksh, describing the collection *When Women Rule* (1985), writes that "Clarke's derogatory and opprobrious depiction of women and the dangers they represent to men may well tempt the reader to see him as a misogynist" (162). Similarly, Daniel Coleman, in a 1998 chapter on masculinity focusing on Joshua Miller-Corbaine from the short-story collection *Nine Men Who Laughed*, writes that "Joshua does not function as a guide to a new masculinity. Simultaneously a producer and a product of capitalist phallocentrism, he perpetuates the system of misogyny that founds his very livelihood" (70). Although Clarke credits the many women in his extended household for raising him and teaching him, his oeuvre highlights repeated episodes of male characters displaying "revulsion coexisting with attraction," as it relates to the women in their lives, a trait David Gilmore, a professor of anthropology, sees as defining many misogynists. He writes: "It seems that wherever we find misogyny, we also find its diametric opposite in equal measure" (203).

In a literary career spanning more than fifty years, Clarke has been essential in characterizing the Black population to itself and to the wider- Canadian society; however, old patterns and tropes repeat themselves, suggesting Clarke's characters have not moved beyond limited constructions of gender. In his last poetry collection, *In Your Crib* (2015), an unnamed youth hopes to use his Mercedes-Benz to attract women, much as Calvin did in "The Motor Car" (1971), written more than forty years earlier. The aging poet who regards the youth outside his window fails to see himself in the youth he criticizes. Clarke's depictions of women, similarly, have evolved only slightly over the course of his career. His latter aging female protagonists are slightly more contemporary versions of his earlier ones. Idora, the struggling mother in the novel *More* (2008), is a reincarnation of a Bernice or Dots from the Toronto Trilogy (1967–75). Mary-Mathilda of *The Polished Hoe* revisits the female inhabitants of the Barbadian sugarcane plantation of *The Survivors of the Crossing*, one of his earliest published novels. What hasn't evolved in Clarke's writing are depictions of complete women, happy and content without men or children in their lives. Aging male characters in Clarke's work fail to take on what Emily Wentzell calls "composite masculinities" as they age; and these rigid gender constructions lead to concomitant restrictions in his older female protagonists as well (26).

Yet, I wonder if "misogyny" is too strong a word to describe Clarke's opus. Certainly, Clarke's aim was not to perpetuate feelings of enmity toward women in his work. And in his last collection of poetry, we see the aging poet, staring out his window, wondering if his "immorality of loud silence" (*In Your Crib* 37) and the invisibility of the lens through which he saw the youth (and I would add women) is somehow responsible for the rudderless place the youth finds himself in. This limited self-criticism, however, gestures toward an enhanced self-knowledge that we did not truly get to see emerge in Clarke's work, as this was his final publication.

Instead, there are several new episodes that echo older ones, leading to misogynistic patterns repeated by the youth, or as the aging poet says, "teaching new dogs old tricks" (*In Your Crib* 37). In "The Motor Car," Barbadian Calvin saves up his money for a Galaxie motor car, which he imagines driving around the West Indian neighbourhood in Toronto so that everyone could admire him with the "Canadian thing" (90)—she is never named—in the passenger seat. Clarke updates the language used to describe women in his last poetry collection but does not change the nature of the discourse. The aging poet criticizes the youth for the way he treats women: "woman and wife became 'hos'; lady labelled 'bitch'" (18), and, "For who had the most of these 'bitches,' are the very ones who grew up to drive machines 'factured by Germans. Calling them 'Rides'" (19) —and the "ride" here refers to both the car and the woman. And just as Calvin does, the youth crashes his motor car, albeit without a "Canadian thing" inside. The aging poet does wonder if the lack of guidance the elders offered the youth is somehow to blame for the repeated patterns: "And you, leaderless, guided only by my silence / mixed with the two-timing urgency of dusk, must walk this next journey by yourself: / with no Elder, no old man, even, Alone. No wisdom / falling out of the skies and the Heavens / to guide you" (52). This lack of guidance offered the youth is precisely the lost opportunity that could have moved him beyond the objectification of women. Gilmore cites education as key in changing men's and boys' attitudes toward women: "The solution, rather, is for elders to alert young men and boys to the nature of their many levels of ambivalence toward women, to raise their consciousness about the duality of their feelings, not only toward women, but toward all things that are important to them" (229). Instead, the old man hides behind his window, saying his "puny words," (49) had he offered them, were insufficient.

Ironically, Clarke has often had women at the centre of his work, which would seem to belie their peripheral status. The importance of such characters as Bernice, Dots, Idora, and Mary-Mathilda does not render them more "complex" than earlier ones. As Clarke's work emerged from the 1970s, we certainly encounter successful women characters of all races; but this success often comes at a very high cost in their lives. These are women who are financially stable, but either morally bankrupt or capitalist pawns, and still needing men or children to complete them. Clemmie, from the short story "Bonanza 1972 in Toronto" (1971), while she has made it financially, is still lonely. She says, "A woman in my position—I have a nice job, I makes a decent wage, and I have a small piece o' land back in Barbados and Canadian Savings Bonds up here—a woman in my position in life should be stepping out with a man who is proud to have walking beside o' him! I should have a regular man" (264). The mother in "They're Not Coming Back" (1993) has a successful job and has jettisoned her cheating husband. But her success has forced her to give up her children to that husband: "The new house was now full of their absence. . . . And the fact that they were not here tonight, welcoming her, as they did every other night, with complaints about the school day and each other, filled her with anxiety" (164). The word "fear" shows up repeatedly in his later work. And when we do encounter a successful, complete woman, Clarke depicts her as mannish, thereby emasculating the men with whom she comes into contact. In the short story "The Discipline" (1985), a Bay Street lawyer is described as "dressed like a man in a three-piece suit. The back of her head and the sweep of her hair make me feel her strength and her force, and I think of her as a man" (2). That there are so few successful, happy, secure women in his work is a telling commentary on his tendency to portray women characters as relying on either men, money, or things to be complete.

In his short-story collection *When Women Rule* (1985), we see Clarke engaging with these ideas of women being erroneously held responsible for the emasculation of the men in their lives, and he claims he titled the collection as he did because he recognized that the women are "deliciously in the background and their influence is not particularly recognized by the men." But he also writes in his unpublished "The West Indian Immigrant in Canada" that

> the black woman has been permitted, through the various exigencies of white racism, to puncture the white society in her role and in her function of servant, maid, cook, hospital nurse, school teacher and so on. This has brought out a subconscious awareness on her part of superiority over her man. The black woman, in certain cases, has flaunted this advantage over her man, in such ways as to crystallize the previous inferiority feelings instilled in his consciousness by the larger society.

By "deliciously" placing women in the background, blaming them for men's emasculation, failing to recognize the entirety of their existences, Clarke perpetuates their diminished status. And Gilmore has written that it is exactly these ambivalent feelings toward women that is the basis of misogyny: "Misogyny stems from unresolved inner conflicts in men," and "a series of multi-layered ambivalences in men lies at the heart of the misogyny affliction" (202).

Clarke's ambivalence toward women highlights the precarious position in which he places his female protagonists. Idora and Mary-Mathilda are his final female protagonists and as such they had the potential to show the evolution of his thinking; however, both women continue to be viewed through the lens of men, incomplete in and of themselves. Idora says, "It is all right, she thinks, even on a Sunday morning, on the way to church, to think about sex. Sex is such a natural thing. Sex is life. Is blood" (*More* 259). Yet Clarke cannot conceive of that sex life without a partner, and a lesbian relationship occurs only if a man is not available. Clarke has Idora flirt with the idea of a relationship with her best friend, Josephine, a relationship they [or he] cannot quite articulate: "And they clasped their arms, for comfort, for explanation, for the greater bond, the greater love, the purer love that two women sometimes share, round each other" (122).

Unfortunately, this example of men-less women falling into convenient affairs is a trope he explored in the 1970s, with Dots and Bernice in the Toronto Trilogy. After Dots and Boysie lose touch with each other in the pursuit of more money and property, Bernice and Dots engage in a careless affair. Despite the forty years between these novels, Clarke seemingly cannot conceive of women being content without men, or women willingly choosing to be in a lesbian relationship.

It might be tempting, however, to view Mary-Mathilda and her mother as moving beyond this male-dominated sexuality by asserting agency over their sex lives, with Mary-Mathilda deciding with whom she will share her bed and her mother encouraging what Jennifer Springer calls "survival pimping." Springer argues that, "in Clarke's narrative, the actions of Mary and her mother, Ma, serve as a political instrument and authoritative voice on the struggles of black women in their attempts to challenge sexual stereotypes while producing a counter-discourse to traditional representations of womanhood through their complex participation in survival pimping and sex work" (171).

Mary-Mathilda becomes the long-term mistress of Mr. Bellfeels, thereby engaging in sex work in an effort to assert her sexuality with the most powerful man in the parish, rather than with any other man who could take her in the canefields when he chooses. Springer says,

> Ma reclaims her own body and that of Mary when she chooses to pimp her daughter in order to secure for her a "better life," one where Mary lives in the plantation great house rather than serve there or work in the neighboring fields. . . . Ma teaches her daughter to tap into her sexual agency, a new understanding of the body, and the varying purposes it can potentially serve—including but not limited to pleasure and economic stability. (175)

But this interpretation of "sexual agency" still privileges men. As Ma says, "Mr. Bellfeels took her, as his right, in his natural arrogance of ownership, as a part of the intricate ritual and arrangement of life on the Plantation" (*The Polished Hoe* 426). If Clarke had chosen to give one of his female protagonists agency over her sexuality, surely it would not have been with that protagonist's own father, a point Mary-Mathilda admits in refusing to call it an "affair": "no, not affair, for it could not be called that, since there was no bargaining power on her part" (426). This is not sexual agency, but rape and incest. Mary-Mathilda's position is not that far removed from the other female plantation workers shown in *The Survivors of the Crossing*, published nearly forty years earlier. And I see in this repeated trope a lack of recognition on Clarke's part, as with the aging poet in his collection *In Your Crib*, of history repeating itself through the continuation of limited constructions of gender and sexuality.

These limited gender roles arise, in part, from a confused conflation of woman as parent and woman as lover and/or wife. The expected dependence on one (woman as parent) can lead to resentment when that dependence continues into adulthood (woman as partner), a point with which Algoo-Baksh concurs:

> Perhaps, too, the negative image of women and their influence presented in *When Women Rule* is inspired in part by Clarke's own emotional troubles, not yet sufficiently digested and absorbed into art. It is also likely that Clarke is exorcizing the sense of dependency on women that he has accumulated through years of reliance on the major women in his life—his grandmother, his mother, and his wife.

A telling example here is the way Clarke similarly describes mother and lover figures in his writing. The following quotation is from an autobiographical piece published in 2014, called "Her Hair is Plaited Tight":

> She sits like a queen. Thick around the hips. Solid around her breasts. Thick and strong down to her long fingernails. And

with her eyes closed. You see her silent, taciturn, like a woman sitting dead in a wooden straight-back chair. But her mighty chest—her "bosom" is the word that she uses—her bosom tells you just the opposite. She is alive. (36)

On first reading, I thought Clarke was describing a love interest, but it turns out the piece is about his mother; it details a letter she received telling her about his father's impending death in the almshouse. In another short story, "A Short Drive" (1992), a young West Indian professor working at Yale falls into a dance with a drag queen, unbeknownst to him. The dancer's body reminds him of his mother: "It was like a mother knowing before the expression of pain is moaned, how to take her child into the safety of her breast and bosom. I sank deep and comfortable in the billows of her love, as her arms wrapped my smaller body in embrace so much like my mother's that I felt I could fall off into a sweet slumber and surrender myself to her" (95). Rather than a kind of Freudian Oedipal love transposed from the mother figure onto a lover, the glorification of, and dependence on, one female figure in Clarke's writing often leads to a confused glorification and dependence on other female figures.

Clarke may or may not have recognized the repetition of certain tropes in his work, but the aged writer in his last poetry collection seems to offer up a recounting of his faults: "I am a man, old of age and disappointment / for the years that passed me by" (*In Your Crib* 42) "I do not have the gift of words / put down in certain rhyme and rhythm, to guide your hand" (45). And he describes his own treatment of the Black youth of the city as "neglect." I would add women to this apology. But surely in acknowledging fault or neglect, Clarke has his aged poet move toward some type of reconciliation, which we, his readers, may have to enact. While the poet does not consider himself among the "elders," merely an "old man," his work can function as a lesson for his readers, and for the youth that he did very much want to reach. The poet's final reckoning, he believes, will be with a higher power: "I will have this discussion, face-to-face, with God / whose heart is larger and much softer / than your compassion" (47).

Perhaps in attempting to depict his characters' misogyny (or his own?), Clarke unwittingly perpetuated it. Jonathan McAloon, whose question opened this paper, does not provide any ready answers about how males can improve their writing about gender. However, he does call for an "open discussion." And I think it is this call for open critique that Clarke's work deserves, not further neglect, which the aged poet calls "unforgivable." The poet's last entreaty asks us to pay attention to what he says, perhaps not what he does: "let me now, as an old man, / rest my heavy, last request: / listen."

Austin Clarke writing.
Permissions: William Ready Division of Archives and Research Collections, McMaster University Library

/CHAPTER 5

That Man, That Man—Stories and Confabulations

Austin Clarke

Austin Clarke's 1986 collection, Nine Men Who Laughed, *includes the stories "A Man" and "How He Do It," both of which offer accounts of Joshua Miller-Corbaine from two perspectives. Miller-Corbaine is a man who dresses and acts the part of a high-powered corporate lawyer but is, in fact, unemployed and entirely dependent on his wife and mistresses for financial support. "A Man" describes Miller-Corbaine's masculine performances in standard English. "How He Does It," written in nation language from the perspective of one of Miller-Corbaine's friends, retells his narrative to further indicate the cracks in his chimerical identity. Both stories offer different takes on performances of masculinity; reading the two in dialogue with one another reveals what can be achieved in these distinct narrative styles.*

This new, previously unpublished story takes up Miller-Corbaine's narrative from a third perspective: that of an embittered white neighbour. In this story Clarke satirizes both Miller-Corbaine's performed masculinity as well as the language and politics of the white society that can only view Black men as con artists, liars, and sexual predators. This new story offers another view on two of Clarke's classic works and some of the major themes in his oeuvre.

The man I want to discuss is a legend. In my neighbourhood at least, and for a short time—the summer of 1987—I expect he was much discussed throughout the city, because his infamy is the subject of a pair of articles, titled "A Man" and "How He Does It," published in consecutive issues of *Saturday Night Magazine*, written by a friend of this fraud, a fellow countryman, a certain Trinidadian by the name of Mr. Austin C. Clarke. Now why, you may ask, would I, an esteemed municipal court judge, squander my time rewriting what was already beaten to death years ago at cocktail parties and around the pool that summer. Well, it's because these two articles about my former neighbour—a certain Mr. Josh M.G. Miller-Corbaine—are satisfyingly revealing, but contradictory, prematurely terminated, and I'd like to expose and correct several important fallacies, which I'm aware of due to my direct involvement in the affair. Moreover, although my name is not actually stated in either article, I am clearly identified as the judge next door, and certain qualities attributed to my person—my supposed unfriendliness for example, the description of my neighbourhood—demand redress. I wrote letters to *Saturday Night*—these were refused; I tried to let the matter drop; but alas, my belief in the supremacy of truth has prompted this account.

First, I'll summarize the articles, indicating the contradictions and making appropriate connections, then I'll explain my role in what happened. The first article is written in plain English. It details the wildly deceitful life that Mr. Miller-Corbaine was leading when he was among us, with four women—all of them white, which is of no importance but for the fact it validates my suspicion that this man is fraudulent and a misogynist. There was his wife, Mary—a lovely, voluptuous woman whom he might as well have beaten so complete was his emotional neglect of her, a fact I was plainly aware of from the moment they arrived in our neighbourhood and he strutted out of that golden hub-capped, silver Cadillac, which he would replace annually with the newest model, to gloat upon their new house from the front lawn his lewd and bulbous eyes, barking indecipherable commands at Mary over his shoulder. Here I'd like to interpose that I was unaware he found me cold, even racist. It's a flagrant lie that we didn't even speak

when a freak snow storm forced us to shovel our own driveways
side by side, and I can only suppose these untruths arise from
his unreasonable cultural-historical resentment of us all. My wife,
Darleen, and I, we consistently invited them to cocktail parties;
and their son, Winchester—or Whinny, as my boy called him—
was welcome at our house any time, we told him that.

We were astonished by this man's vulgarity. He was the type
who would lean into the horn rather than step out of his car to
ring a doorbell. He carried on his person his weight in gold, in
his teeth, around his fingers and wrists, and no matter what the
occasion he wore a three-piece suit and a starched white shirt
so criss-crossed with gold watch-chains he called to mind one of
those heavily ornamented Clydesdales at the Royal Agricultural
Winter Fair (which, incidentally we invited them to once, only to
have that man spook a team by tossing his program out of the box
just as they were clopping past). And wherever he went he would
carry a thick, black-leather briefcase with his initials, every last one
of them (J.M.G.M.—C.) burnt in gold. He informed me when we
first chatted that he was a corporate lawyer, but when I told him I
was a judge, I observed that even his dark complexion showed red
and he began to sweat. I understood then and there—at that very
first cocktail party they attended—that I'd trapped him in a lie.
And my resolve to expose him would harden with time.

The first of the two articles purports to expose many basic
facts—some of which I know, *prima facie*, to be false. I'll list them
quickly. He lived in a well-to-do neighbourhood. True. Our neighbourhood is very close to Forest Hill Village—it meanders along
the west brow of the Cedarvale ravine. But I contest the insular-
ity that Mr. Clarke implies, suggesting we're an island of prigs
and racists. Our neighbourhood, our street, ends at Bathurst. If
you cross Bathurst, take Claxton two blocks to Kenwood, turn
left there, one block over you'll find Vaughn Rd., famous for its
Jamaican character. Moreover, I'd like to admit, "as evidence for
the defence," that I happily take lunch, *to stay*, at Albert's Jamaican
Food Restaurant with my son, and have done so for years; so that

Albert says "hello" when he sees me and one of the five surly women who serve there sometimes smile.

Since we're on the subject of our neighbourhood, I'd also like the reader to know that, unlike the one portrayed in the first article, which is hostile with nosy neighbours peeking from behind curtains and front yards empty and unfriendly except for automatic sprinklers, the neighbourhood we live in is actually among the safest and most friendly in the city. I can walk to the store on Bathurst for a litre of milk on a warm Saturday morning, when cicadas are already singing in the tops of powerful maple trees, and not only do all my neighbours smile and children bike safely to and from the ravine with joyous peals of laughter, Mrs. Chong and I share a warm rapport and underprivileged children frequently (and lucratively) hold car washes at the corner gas station. Mr. Miller-Corbaine was such a problem not because he was black, not even because he was so unapologetically crude; no, we found him such a problem because he was an aggressive, reckless driver, and we wondered if he intentionally swerved to strike our children off their bikes with his Cadillac.

Men of a common profession know each other instinctively, and they can smell a phoney from a long way away, especially when the profession is the law, when you work for truth and justice. Both articles—the second is written in pidgin and has even more inaccuracies than the first—reveal unequivocally that this man is no lawyer, which I already knew and had brought to the attention of Mary. She blushed and begged me to keep quiet. The first article indicates that he spent his days leering at women from his car and from a coffee shop on Bloor St., when he wasn't carrying on with a nubile doting schoolteacher, or a pathetic retiree whom he'd stopped sleeping with when she had reached 49, or a rich Jewess who lived on other side of Forest Hill—of course, unbeknownst to each other and to his wife.

He lived off his wife. Her father was a company man, she was a school teacher, a fine, liberal-minded woman with a handsome build who taught social studies and ethnic culture. His son, who obviously resented that awful man and spent all the time he could with our boy, Tim, attended Upper Canada College. He was nothing like his father, and my boy still talks to him occasionally. The fact is he treated his wife like a maid and I resented it. I resented that Jewish princess he brought over when his wife was away, flaunting and snapping shots of her on the lawn in front of the house. The first article indicates I was raking my "immaculate" lawn when that happened—it was covered in leaves, the photos would confirm that this happened in fall, not summer—and that I retreated into my house disapprovingly. I did, I certainly did, and from the living room window I determined I would find out the truth, no matter what.

In the second article, Mr. Clarke involves himself, using his native tongue. The pidgin's vague, the grammar and spelling, willfully incorrect; nevertheless, it becomes clear that he's reneging on what's said in the earlier article about the young teacher whom Mr. Miller-Corbaine violated once a month, "after that time," and Mr. Clarke substitutes himself instead, playing up the po-boy from the Islands who dumbly types information into legal documents for his spurious friend, hoping on a wing and a prayer that he actually is a "bona fide" lawyer, like he says he is. In that article, Mary goes to the Jewess to confront her (instead of discovering in her own living room, as in the first article), and we think Mr. Miller-Corbaine is sunk, but the little weasel—he looks like one, the way he slinks about with sloped shoulders—pulls the wool over the Jew's eyes, convincing her with the help of ingenuous Whinny that Mary's merely an unstable domestic; meanwhile convincing Mary that he'll henceforth be faithful to her.

This all happened. I know because I'd been following the case ever since the afternoon I saw him take that tramp's photograph on the front lawn, and I crept over and watched them through the living room window, him almost passed out in his three piece suit and her naked like a two-bit whore, staring at a picture of gentle Mary on the wall. I saw it and I heard Mary and the boy get home and watched her drop both valises when she opened the door; and she crumbled into tears, grabbed Whinny's hand and fled to our house. Then and there I vowed to ruin that man. I knew Mary would forgive him, and my blood boiled. The question is, how do you sink a man who's just the shell of a man. You push him down in a spot that would drown a normal man, and he pops right up, laughs and floats away. That's what happened after Mary discovered him with the naked Jew— although the article ends without saying so—and that's what happened when I gave her the address and she confronted that woman in her apartment.

"Your dinner's getting cold, judge" (a little joke between the wife and I), Darleen called from the kitchen. I hushed her and wouldn't come away from the window. I stayed until after midnight, going over it again and again, three versions of the same story, raging by degrees. So far as I could piece together, he'd won, he'd got off scot-free and would continue pursuing his malignant ways with impunity. Darleen asked me to turn off the light and I said, "No, I'm not finished." I need to defeat that man who lives next door to me, who threatens our children with his menacing Cadillac. And the truth should be enough, the neighbours' sound judgment, or those tramps. I could follow him to their homes and expose him. But he's already been exposed! Nothing has happened, he doesn't care, they don't want to know badly enough.

Where's justice? What about men, rock-solid men, who work hard for a living, are faithful, who don't dare strike a woman or disabuse a child? His colour's not the issue—why must they always make colour the issue? What difference does it make? He owes no apologies for his violent compatriots and their drugs and guns if he comes to live in my neighbourhood respectfully. But I don't like my fundamental principles flaunted, and I don't like leeches. How can I sink him? I screamed. Why are his jaundiced eyes yellow? What does he expect from me?

The only way to drown a hollow man is to scuttle him or mark him permanently for what he denies. I planned a cocktail party to that end.

I sometimes wonder if the second article is a takeoff, a hoax. It's got some important details that are missing from the first, but the tone's so different, it's not at all the same, and in it he's a teetotaler, which is patently false. Mr. Miller-Corbaine's a heavy drinker, I can attest to that. I was depending on it for my design to win the day.

I invited Mr. Miller-Corbaine and Mary one hour early, and I told the wait staff to make his drinks strong. He was sweating brilliantly by the time the others arrived, though he still refused to surrender to me even one piece of his suit, and he greeted everyone with nuts in his teeth. Rhonda arrived last.

Rhonda's a black whore. I had instructed her to dress to allure, but with style, and to be sweet to Mr. Miller-Corbaine, whom I struggled to describe until she said, "You mean he's black, right?" Right. I also detailed the layout of the bottom floor of our house, and the erstwhile maid's room off the kitchen. At ten o'clock she strutted in on sharp yellow shoes. I introduced her to the guests as a newly minted lawyer whom I'd mentored. She was scintillating and gracious, a fine young hooker, and when I finally presented her to Mr. Miller-Corbaine, Mary was sticking close; but such was Rhonda's charm, Mary would soon be blushing and working to compensate for her initial frigidity with ingratiating smiles. I left everyone to mingle.

Some hours later—two perhaps—I decided I'd better distract Mary. I said to her, "Join me on the porch and I'll smoke a cigar. I'll chuckle with panache and indicate broken boards in the fence between our yards." Mary nodded and tried to excuse herself, so I said something complimentary about Whinny. Meanwhile, Mr. Miller-Corbaine was laughing, baring his gilt teeth, and Rhonda was touching his shoulder, then his leg. Outside, I repeated myself, "Our fence is rotten, let's have a new one built, more elegant. And what a fine boy Whinny is." I watched Rhonda take Mr. Miller-Corbaine by the arm to the maid's room. I shivered and remarked upon the cold.

Mary was distressed when she didn't see her husband as soon as we re-entered the house. I suggested to her that her husband must have gone home to bed. She hurried away to see. In the meantime, a climax was mounting, a proper resolution, so I collected a few of the neighbours' men and one wife and let it be known I had a very special bottle of overproof rum waiting in the adjacent room that they might like to sample. They liked. Follow me. They followed. I opened the door—after you—and *ta-daaa*, I turned on the light.

It was even better than I had imagined. Mr. Miller-Corbaine was on his knees, pressed in behind her. Her dress was up almost over her head (she looked like a black-eyed Susan). Luckily for her, her buttocks were partly covered by his crumpled shirttails. Both of them simply stared at us and blinked. "Mr. Miller-Corbaine!" my wife, who was with us, belatedly cried. He squirmed a very uncomfortable smile, tugging at Rhonda's dress. Rhonda's eyes narrowed, her lip hooked a sneer—my neighbours and I shuffled backwards.

I thought, Mary must be back, and went out to intercept her. She needs to see this, she has to know! "I can't find him," Mary said. "Mary, I don't know what to say."

I hinted at what was in the room, tried to hold her, but she had to see for herself, which was best. She saw, she exclaimed, she fled.

Now that's that. I'm entirely satisfied: Mr. Miller-Corbaine has been fully exposed to anyone who matters, and my memory preserves this tableau. I shall usher the others out of the room, and I'll toss Mr. Miller-Corbaine a blanket off a shelf in the closet. "Cover yourself up," I'll sneer, switching the light off before I close the door.

CHAPTER 6

Burrowing Into the Craft: Editing Austin Clarke

Dennis Lee

Dear Paul,

What can I tell you about working with Austin? We lived a block away from each other, that's one thing—on Brunswick Avenue, near Sibelius Park in central Toronto. And for maybe three months in 1970, we were pretty much parked in each other's back pockets.

Austin's novels had been published by big houses. But he'd turned to Anansi with his first story collection, *When He Was Free and Young and He Used to Wear Silks*. He showed it to us for two reasons. The accepted wisdom was that a book of short stories carried the commercial kiss of death, so doors were mostly closed elsewhere. And he had acquired a reputation as such a difficult author to deal with that (as I understood it) one or more of his previous publishers wanted nothing more to do with him. My memory is that Graeme Gibson had met him, and urged him to give Anansi a try.

So Austin passed me the manuscript—and I loved it. I read it in a kind of pure, context-free way: I'd never made short stories a focus in my reading or studying, and I didn't pretend to know much about the history of the form, its place in Canadian letters, or really anything beyond what happened in my nervous system when I read the stories. And the freedom, the *zing*, the sure-footedness—along with the insight into West Indian lives in Canada, specifically Toronto—made it a done deal. Anansi *had* to publish this book. We were three years old, we were a writers' press, and we were too dumb to know what would sell and what wouldn't.

So we started honing in on specific stories right away. That may have taken Austin by surprise—I don't know if things worked that way with his previous publishers. I can't remember if we even had a formal contract for writers at that point; anyway, the whole focus was on making a wonderful piece of work even better. With some stories, I made only a few copy-editing suggestions; they didn't need any work. But with others, I raised serious questions about—well, about whatever; I can't call back the specifics now. And there were discussions about which stories to keep and which to lose, and what the best sequence would be.

In truth, it was a much lighter editing job than with many Anansi titles, where in those days we were often publishing an author's first book. Clarke was already more accomplished than that. But from his side of things, it was probably more than he'd been subjected to elsewhere—and moreover, conducted as one writer to another. It was two scribblers, burrowing into the craft.

Austin rose to the occasion like nobody's business. He put everything else aside, and worked on the manuscript story by story. He was far from accepting every suggestion I made, but he engaged with my questions, and did whatever rewriting he felt was called for. Did it intently, with good grace, and quickly. I also remember him telling me he had one more story he wanted to include, but he hadn't written it yet; it might be too experimental to be acceptable. . . . He launched into it anyway, and soon enough brought it over—and it knocked me out. It was fantastic. Not only did we hustle it into the book, it became the title story.

So working with Austin was the exact opposite of everything I'd heard. He wasn't a diva, he didn't create childish self-indulgent scenes, he didn't test me and others at Anansi with unreasonable demands. We did serious literary work together, and he was a class act—as much as any Anansi author I'd worked with.

And then in 1971, the book was published. It looked handsome, we were all delighted—no problems. But immediately, Austin shifted gears. He started treating me and the Anansi staff (most of them working for nothing, in our grimy basement digs) like his private help. I couldn't believe the transformation. A lot of it was just his manner; I don't remember any cosmic publishing showdowns. But abruptly, the laser-focused craftsman and colleague-in-words had become a jerk who addressed his close collaborators of a few weeks previous as if they were slow-witted servants. I'm sure it was a defensive reflex he'd adopted for many years by then, to cope with the racism he met in Canada. You can't judge his behaviour apart from the mistreatment he'd experienced at the hands of bigots. So it's understandable from that viewpoint. But after we'd worked together with such mutual respect and co-operation, it was a drag to deal with. In retrospect, I'm glad I got to see Austin at his best to begin with—as a wholly committed writer of stature. That made it a shock when he reverted to the superior airs, but some of his publishers had probably seen nothing but those airs.

Austin's subsequent books went to other publishers, which had always been the assumption when we did *Free and Young*. And while we overlapped at literary gatherings from time to time, we never had an occasion to move back into that deep collaboration. Austin had a line, though, that he liked to produce at those events. It was a combo of the provocateur and the fellow craftsman. "This is Dennis Lee," he'd say, introducing me to people I already knew. "He was my editor once." His eyes would sparkle wickedly. "And he was the worst slave-driver known to man." He'd wait to see if he'd baited anybody's liberal guilt with that one. But at the same time, there was a recognition I felt too—that we'd worked hard together, in the service of a marvellous book, and it was a good thing to have shared that for a while.

Cheers,
Dennis

CHAPTER 7

Editorial Notes for "When He Was Free and Young and He Used to Wear Silks"

Dennis Lee

Austin,

This can be in its way the most exciting story in the book; but it will have to <u>become</u> that. At the moment, candidly, it both revs you up a great deal and lands on its nose. What I suggest is not taking fewer chances in it, but taking <u>more</u>; accepting that you're into a new kind of writing here, and going whole hog with it. You can write this way; and it takes as much skill & craft as a traditional story does; and the result will be good enough that you can afford to take the time over it.

I wonder if you would be willing to do one rewrite first, and then let us talk over that draft? The responses I have to this story are more intuitive and apply to the whole story: there is very little point—as there was with all the other stories—to making line-by-line comments at this stage. I have two general reactions:

(1) The situation. I read the book as a series of improvisations on a very simple theme or situation. I assume that, while it isn't intended to be laid out clearly in the first paragraph, I

am supposed to get the shape of the situation fairly clearly on the way through. I don't, though. I make out a guy, A.C., who has hung around with the artists at the Pilot 5 years ago, back there having a drink with a poetess and her husband (maybe not him?) with whom she's breaking up, or has broken up, A.C. and she nearly made it 5 years back? And he is comparing her now with Marian, and is glad he has Marian. Right? But . . . to toss out a few of my bewilderments . . . who did he spy on the "summerstreet"? Is Marian now in Toronto? Is his memory of her on Yonge Street of a time in the recent past? . . . And generally with the white girl, what's the context of their getting together?

I also wonder whether more of the social scene mightn't come out fragmentarily and indirectly—about his life 5 years ago, changes for him, for the artistic scene, the Pilot, the girl. You could fill in (impressionistically) a whole panorama of a man's life and a city's life and a subculture's life, just by evoking things in straight phrases.

(2) The style. This is what I want you to take seriously most of all. You can do breathtaking things here—you have already done some of them. But there is also a lot of swoopy, breathless, throw-the-pieces-up-in-the-air-and-hope, good old-fashioned faking it. Re-read it; you'll know what I mean every time you come to it. What I conjecture happened is that you wrote this in a burst; and, since it propels a long way farther technically than your other writing, most other people's writing (I can imagine Hugh Garner tackling this one!), it may have seemed that since you were breaking all the rules, you might as well have the full binge. But—as the best passages indicate—you've scrapped one set up of rules and taken up another set. I don't know what they are in doctrinal terms; but I do know that in impulsive, lyrical writing like this it is more important than in any other kind of writing not to fake it. Because the reader is looking for the purple, or the places where giddy phrase-making is being used to sneak by without feeling

through the substance of the lines; and if he finds any of that he is going to dismiss the whole thing—not just notice a little slip in the tone.

I also wonder whether the really dithyrambic tone wouldn't be best held mostly in check till the Marian passages. They paid a little because the whole story is written at virtually the same pitch and tempo. There might be more changes, arabesques, textures on the way through within this swirling stream of consciousness—basically, beginning in several more prosaic modes and accelerating into this beautiful celebration of a woman (though—again—gone thru ruthlessly by you now from this distance).

End of lecture. This is the only story in the whole collection where I blow the whistle and bid-and-beseech you to dig back into the first principles of what you've written—in all the other ones you've already realised that so thoroughly that we've basically been re-arranging final details on the surface, even where they were fairly important details. But I think this is the only story that is still in the process of getting born; listening to an editor-as-midwife is both harder and more useful than to an editor-as-mosaic-polisher—listen to Graeme on the score. But this is the only story in the lot where a midwife is relevant. So PUSH!

Dennis

CHAPTER 8

Sometimes, a Motherless Child: A Double Take

Giovanna Riccio

Entrance

They embraced, touching bodies, and slapping each other on the back three times, as if they belonged to an old fraternity of rituals and mystery. They let go of each other, and did it a second time, with their heads touching each other's shoulders. It was Italian and it was African and it was this that joined them in their close friendship these past nine years. They saw each other every day, either at school or here in BJ's room. (Austin Clarke, "Sometimes, a Motherless Child," 1992)

BJ, it's me, Marco, primed for closing day at Woodbine. I've got the *Globe and Mail* and *Racing Forum*. Let's drink vodka and listen to *A Love Supreme*—scrutinize and add to our winnings.

BJ, come on man, answer the door. It's cold and the longer I stand, the more I feel guilty about us skipping school and lying. *Dai*—my mother's croonin' in my head as she fills the kitchen with tomato sauce smells and the sizzle of veal cutlets crinkling in olive oil: *Oggi?* She asks—Today? How school was? *Fai lu bravo*—be a good boy—make your mamma proud. You know when you were born, you *papà* who work so hard laying bricks, his hands all rough, the skin all thick and cracked—you no gonna have hands like him—he look at you; you a *bello bambino* right from the start—born *dolce come un angelo*—a sweet angel. You *papà* he take you tiny hands that open like a newborn dream, 'n smiley, he say—all serious in good Italian, like he blessing you with prophecy—"Felice, queste sono le mani di un dottore"—these are the hands of a doctor.

I remember the beatin' you got the first time we cut class when we were just ten. After that, your mom got the landlord to keep an eye on you. He's out there each morning, checking for your footsteps in the snow lining the lane out your apartment. It didn't take you long though—to step out, coat over your PJs, then back in, planting each foot exactly into the dark ghosts your shoes pressed into that cold, white betrayal.

Your mom's none wiser, headin' out each morning early to her housekeeper job. So proud of your report cards, and how good you're lookin'; still making you lunch at eighteen and clippin' a five dollar bill to the bag; layin' plans for you the way my pop lays bricks. Mixin' her hard work with your future; maybe she saw a doctor in your hands too.

Greeting

BJ smiled. He turned Coltrane up. The car was filled once more with the beauty of music, with the pulse of emotion, the feeling of the time: and they remained quiet in the waves of the melodious tune they both liked so much and argued about. BJ insisted, because of his new religion, that it was a religious chant, Marco, equally insistent, said it was a love song.

"A love supreme," He began chanting. "A love supreme. Nineteen times the brother says a love supreme! Nineteen times, BJ!" He never lacked enthusiasm about this aspect of the song. (Austin Clarke)

But praise God, he doesn't own a car. A car is the surest thing to make a police shoot a black man dead. (BJ's mother)

Penance

BJ, you were something else. All those books, you were like a walking 'cyclopedia, man. And also a genius at the track. Dragging on a Gauloise, all bohemian-intellectual, drinking vodka and OJ. That morning, I could see *The Autobiography of Malcolm X* where you'd been sitting reading, a strip of Kente cloth marking the page. All those shelves, lined with books; all that Black power.

Something in your voice though—when you said, *Today's the last day.* We were smokin', had our best year yet. We made thousands each plus our combined kitty and it was all your figuring: "Concentration and dedication," you preached, "we are investors, don't ever bet on longshots, longshots are for racetrack touts."

You warned me that it wasn't safe driving to the track—meaning it wasn't safe for a Black guy and an Italian to be driving that kind of car. I can still hear you askin', "Have you told your parents you own a white BMW, more correctly, a fifty-percent share in a late-model white BMW?" Because I insisted, "BJ, man, what's the point of havin' wheels if we're stuck on the TTC?" And because you loved our classy car, loved speedin' on the 401, our vanity plates yelling BLUE . . .

"Only because it's the last day, Marco," you agreed, "because it's the last day."

War Requiem for BJ

Chorus:
BJ's unsettled spirit patrols Toronto's
circled city. What was his crime? Breathing
while Black; no rest where haunted cop-lights shine.

Mother:
A shaky goodbye spoils each day's
parting; grave our hearts, pounding out prayer:
whose night tears up as sirens wail?

This day handcuffed to death:
licensed breach, billy clubs, bullets
—BJ's broken, blood-soaked body.
No need to cover up this end
foretold in newspapers over
and over on spattered screens.
Though Justice reels, conned, battered
we rise to weigh and render—We!
No rest 'till there accounting be.

Marco
No rest this day when a scarlet night
eclipses its hunted sun; unshackle tongues,
sound BJ's song—ring no passing bell.
—Instead let squad cars light
this shattered, shrouded, street,
let sirens be his passing bell.
What's law if chance be branded in skin
what's a Black life if force spins red
and cruisers rev to bleach the streets?
Suspended in his timeless cell
lone memory burned in BJ's eyes
penned, he paced and paced until
Malcolm's voice abolished walls,
his speech set free metallic fear.
Plain clothes walked him from reverie
to a blue, unmarked car—Iago's white heat;
then under dispatched snow, night sticks
sundering stars, guns scripting shadow.

Austin Clarke
This story I have wrought primed by bodies
buried in margins—margins fleshed in words
so lines take on blood and hold,
No rest—let no shade go untold.

CHAPTER 9

"These Virtues o' the Cullinerry Harts": Talking Food and Politics in the Letters of Austin Clarke, Sam Selvon, and Andrew Salkey

Kris Singh

Austin Clarke begins his culinary memoir, *Pig Tails 'n Breadfruit*, with a declaration that resonates with many a Caribbean reader: "Food. It is a word that defines my life" (1). This line came to mind as I reflected on my relationship with my grandmother and how frequently we talk about food, whether it is about how hospitality for us Trinidadians involves feeding our guests, her steadfast belief in the power of offering food to *murtis*, or the first time she slit a goat's throat to satisfy her husband's appetite. It is not that she has a particular fascination with food. Rather, it is that food is the language through which her care, knowledge, experience, and personality can flow to me. At the same time, her relationship to food is shaped by the political forces defining her life. In January 2016, for example, the prime minister of Trinidad and Tobago engaged in a clumsy attempt to prioritize the local agricultural economy by lambasting the attendees of a Chamber of Industry and Commerce dinner. He singled out the women: "The average woman in this room cannot peel a cassava" (Clyne). Prime Minister Rowley served up a clear example of how women are positioned as caretakers of culinary knowledge and as meal providers. He was shifting public emphasis from larger political decisions mostly made by men to what he saw as the personal shortcomings of women. These two instances exemplify a point Clarke has frequently made in his work: food is personal and political. Its preparation informs intimate family relationships as it reinforces gendered divisions of labour. Its availability influences an individual's access to a balanced diet, just as it determines a nation's balance of trade. Its discourse—the stories, jokes, knowledge, and history that circulate with it—shapes individual and collective identities.

Clarke's *Pig Tails* is explicitly aimed at exploring how the roles of food in his life, in Barbadian culture more broadly, and in the Caribbean's history of slavery are all intertwined. In addition to the explicit focus of *Pig Tails*, much of his fiction foregrounds the personal, cultural, and colonial entanglements of food. In his description of Caribbean immigrants in his Toronto Trilogy, for instance, he describes characters who nostalgically yearn for home-cooked food, and others who have a knack for finding the necessary "ingreasements" in their new home. Yet, these characters must also deal with the stereotype of being "born cooks" and therefore naturally suited for domestic labour.

Clarke's consideration of food suffuses not only his published work but his personal correspondence with Sam Selvon and Andrew Salkey; food becomes a basis of exchange in this male network of letters.[1] During his Bajan boyhood, Clarke's Sunday lunches were regularly paired with Selvon's storytelling via the BBC Radio program *Caribbean Voices*. They eventually met in London in 1965, when Clarke was visiting as a freelance radio broadcaster for CBC and their correspondence began shortly thereafter and continued as Selvon moved with his family to Calgary in 1978. Salkey, whose communication with Clarke also began in the mid-1960s and whom Clarke affectionately calls Handrew, moved from Jamaica to Britain in 1952. His work with *Caribbean Voices*, his co-founding of the Caribbean Artists Movement, and his novels, poetry, travelogues, and editing work established him as a prominent literary figure. As with Selvon, a move to Canada features in his early letters to Clarke. On August 2, 1965, he writes, "Look man, the Canada thing has really bitten me and my wife. She hasn't stopped talking a) about you and b) about Canada. She approves of both of you, especially of Canada for me, even for a brief spell on the Fellowship thing if it even comes off." This plan was never actualized, but Salkey moved to Hampshire College in Massachusetts in 1976; throughout these relocations, all three authors maintained regular communication. Clarke commemorates the "triangular literary route" of these letters in *A Passage Back Home: A Personal Reminiscence of Samuel Selvon*, published upon Selvon's death in 1994. In that memoir, Clarke notes, "Handrew bears an even bigger love for Sam. . . . I would not mention Sam's name in three letters; and Handrew would want to know why? Did I hear from Sam-Sam? Was he all right? Was his health holding up? Was he writing?" (129). In what was undoubtedly a heavy blow to Clarke, Salkey passed away almost exactly a year after Selvon.

Clarke, Salkey, and Selvon partake in a form of epistolary *picong* that shares some of the improvisational skill and cultural knowledge of the kitchen talk that Clarke details in *Pig Tails* as well as some of the characteristic bravado, self-deprecation, affection, and humour that constitutes Caribbean "ole talk." If we were to take Selvon at his word, he and Clarke were just "two big literary giants sitting down, one in the East and one in the West, pelting one another with shit instead of getting down to the serious business of creating Literature!" (August 12, 1982). Shooting the shit or not, their correspondence took on a familiar flavour, as culinary references pepper their epistles. A recurring metaphor is that of money as bread, but often with a Caribbean twist, as when Clarke triumphantly announces, on June 20, 1980, "Bread like peas!" This phrase riffs on the more familiar saying "licks like peas," or a good licking. Pigeon peas, of course, are abundant when in season; and so, too, when you receive a happy financial windfall in lean times, it seems plentiful. Salkey, however, in a letter dated July 10, 1972, reminds Clarke of island nuance when it comes to peas:

> Make me take first things first, nuh. Who tell you say that we Jamaickans call f'we rice an' peas "peas an' rice." You make mistake man. Is Trickidadians who say peas an' rice. Not we! We born an' grow sayin' rice an' peas, always Jamaickan rice an' peas. We even got a whole complex o' different rice an' peas dishes to rass clate! We got red peas rice an' peas, gunggu peas rice an' peas, split peas rice an' peas, an' so on, papa! So don't fuck wit' we an' confuse we wit' Little Eric people them a blood!!!

In both serious and playful ways, Salkey displays close attention to national and regional identities in his letters. Here, his reference to Eric Williams, the first prime minister of Trinidad and Tobago, demonstrates how his comedic turns, which were rarer than Selvon's and Clarke's, usually feature in more explicit, extended political discussions.

Salkey often relayed to Clarke not just the latest election result or policy decision but also the quality of his peers' political sensibilities. On April 28, 1970, he laments, "The boys fucking up with all sorts of imported mouthings, and not thinking natively, at all, at all. Every time I turn either Marcuse lick me, or some out of date Marx, or some stale Cleaver that even Eldridge himself would disown." Yet Salkey was not one for distanced condescension. He staunchly believed in community building and organized activism. He says in the same letter,

> But, papa, they, over here, stale and pretentious, but I working solidly with them and giving them hell all the same. We just got extremely bashed about by the police in Hyde Park last Sunday. We marched on our Trinidad question, and we take over from another march on Vietnam with some English Marxists, and

the police arrest twenty-five of us, and kill we with beating. I
manage to fuck one straight in the face with a hard fist, and
duck him, when he tried to arrest me. It was a bitch!

Salkey prioritized local action that worked in tandem with
transnational movements toward justice. The "Trinidad question" refers to the militarized crackdown by the PNM[2] government on what was framed as young people mimicking the radical
Black Power politics of elsewhere. W. Chris Johnson details this
history in his article "Guerrilla Ganja Gun Girls: Policing Black
Revolutionaries from Notting Hill to Laventille," in which he
discusses the National United Freedom Fighters in Trinidad
alongside the protests in Notting Hill and in Sir George Williams
University in Montreal. When situated within this larger political history, Salkey's letters in effect detail his participation in
the "community of black liberation movements in England" in
the 1960s and '70s (Johnson 286). Johnson explains that this
community was "an electric latticework of people and ideas
that coursed through homes and neighbourhoods, shattering
and fusing organizations, trespassing across cities and national
borders" (286). He adds special emphasis to the role of gender
and sexuality in these movements, considering Althea Jones-
Lecointe; her mother, Viola; and her sisters, Beverley and
Jennifer. Jones-Lecointe features in the Clarke-Salkey correspondence as Salkey updates Clarke on the circumstances that
preceded the landmark Mangrove Nine trial. On July 13, 1970,
Salkey reiterates to Clarke that "John La Rose and I have staked
our lives on our work in the community, not only as writers but
as workers and common blood to all Black people in Britain."
However, once again, he condemns the lack of support from his
peers: "You see all like George Lamming, V.S. Naipaul, Wilson
Harris, and even Samuel Selvon (a sweet brother though he is)!
None of them ever bothers to come into the mainstream of the
struggle and help out, you know." He contrasts the "selfishness"
of these writers with his commitment: "Right out front, taking all

the fucking blows and getting our names in the MI5, Scotland Yard, U.S. Embassy and High Commission lists are the same ol' pavement fighters: John La Rose, Jeff Crawford, a vanguard of two students at the Centre, and yours truly" (July 13, 1970). It is clear that while Salkey worried about what was lacking amongst those around him in London, he perceived Clarke to be as politically astute, engaged, and savvy as himself. Much like the communal space that was the Mangrove Restaurant, the epistolary space Salkey and Clarke carved out afforded vital expressions of joy, anger, and solidarity.

Through the decades, Salkey and Clarke invite each other into discussions about political developments in England, Barbados, Jamaica, Canada, Ghana, Libya, South Africa, and elsewhere. A juxtaposition of two such conversations highlights these writers' cognizance that anti-Black racism does not emerge spontaneously but through longer histories. In a letter dated June 19, 1970, Salkey gives a play-by-play commentary on the UK elections as Edward Heath surprises all in defeating Harold Wilson. He notes, "Well, papa, here I am at 12:25 midnight, into the day after the British polling stations are closed and the counting and results are going on round me like peas." He moves on to discuss his progress with writing *Georgetown Journal* but cannot help but return to the elections a few paragraphs later: "Time: 12:45 am Friday 19th June. Jesus! Winston Spencer Churchill, Churchill grandson just get elect, the radio say. . . . But what happen now that Enoch Party going rule the country?" His agitation mounts as he conveys the results of a few more constituencies and ends with the prickling prediction that "Is nothing but pass card and detention catch Black people, now, in White Britain."

Salkey's reporting exposes the political environment confronting Black writers in England in this era. A decade later, by which time Salkey was situated in Massachusetts, Clarke comments on the latest election result. On November 10, 1980, he writes, "Reagan get in! Um going to be pressure in black people arse from now onwards christian soldiers! <u>Rax-rax-rax</u>! I like I getting frighten to come down there in January yuh! Reagan isn't no sweetbread. Reagan believe in mekking Amurca strong again; and when Amurca strong, the brothers going-be catching shite." The meaning of Reagan's success is as clear to Clarke as Heath's was to Salkey. These were the latest iterations of a longer history of anti-Black racism, and they had to make sense of each noxious development. Though Clarke's appeal to that favoured English hymn may be facetious, his fright is real. Yet he makes room to write with style, remaining assured of Salkey's enjoyment of it and somehow mitigating the dread evoked by the news. These letters serve as warnings and acknowledgements of real threats, but the tone is not one of despair.

An extended passage from Clarke illuminates how their letters and friendship sustained them over the years. On March 20, 1987, Clarke was in the throes of writing *More* after a spell of inertia. He exclaims,

> For had I not been possessed of a strength poured into my veins by Gladys Luke, my mother, long ago, and had been affected by the tenuous philosophy of life of North Americans, I would have given hope to the winds, drunk a thousand sleeping pills, or else commit some other stupidly heinous act. But the fish head soup, and the Bible; the boil' chicken in rice, and the Bible; the green banana and mackerel, and the Bible; the sheep head soup with the eyes staring at you, and the Bible; pulp' eddoes and herring, and the Bible; split-pea soup and dumplings and salt beef and pig tails and sweet potato, and the Bible; cou-cou and h'arslick, and the Bible, cou-cou and salt fish, and the Bible; and breadfruit cou-cou and Bajan stew, and the fucking Bible, is what have me here this blessed Sarduh morning.

Clarke often offered such introspection, and it is clear that he is underscoring not the nutritional value of food but the traditions, the relationships, the values, and the love implied. Brinda Mehta in "The Mother as Culinary Griotte," explains that in *Pig Tails*

Clarke uses food and his mother's preparation of food to show that "food production permits black Barbadian women to assert their selfhood through their subjective claiming of Caribbean history. Food becomes a signifier of cultural consciousness and a subsequent affirmation of a mode of cultural production that has its roots in a disenfranchising history of slavery and oppression" (327). Clarke's improvised culinary riffs reflect and reproduce those affirmations. What is being trafficked in Clarke's writerly whims often drew Salkey's honest appreciation: "Got two wonderful letters from you today. Brilliantly witty. Splendidly salty. Loved them both" (March 11, 1982). Salkey expresses a similar appreciation of Clarke's fiction, explaining, "I like your work papa. It clean & strong & full of power because it is so people-centred" (March 6, 1972). Wordplay for its own sake was never enough for Salkey. Public and private writing had to do more, and what these letters do is centre intimacy as a political act. Yes, these letters show a healthy trade of articles, newspaper clippings, and books across national borders and across continents. Yes, there is an urgent exchange of appointments, letters of recommendation, and opportunities that are vital to the writer's fiscal well-being. Yes, there is commentary on elections, assassinations, and protests. Yes, there is mentorship, mutual advising, and peer review. But the intimacy borne and nurtured through these letters is as political as the circumstances that demand them. In bearing witness to each other's achievements and failures, glee and anger, fears and jokes about those fears, they find the salve of knowing that one is not alone and that one's work is read by those with the cultural and historical sense that match one's own.

As noted before, Salkey did not find the same political commitment or awareness in Selvon, though he remained close to him. On June 19, 1972, Salkey considers Selvon's upcoming teaching position in San Diego, and tells Clarke,

Advice him about the mood of the young people them, about their political thing, about their world view and so on. Poor Sam, he been lock away for a long time, and he sort of ol' fashion in him thinking and ways. He hardly know anything about Fanon, Malcolm, Cleaver, Angela, or for that matter about Che, Ho, Giap, or about Vietnam, Algiers, Cuba, or anything in that line. . . . He don't attend to Blackness or radical politics or nothing.

Salkey is often blunt about Selvon's deficiencies while championing his strengths as a writer. Perhaps, Selvon's East Indian–West Indian positioning meant that he enjoyed the privilege of representing Black immigrants in his fiction—and being lauded for it— without having to engage in a full-throated fight against anti-Black racism outside his writerly life. Salkey's comments invite a re-interrogation of Selvon's depiction of Black activism in works like *Moses Ascending*, published in 1975.

The exchanges captured in these letters make clear that all three authors stood ready to aid each other. To borrow their parlance, they knew that bread is good when you can get it and even better if you can trade it in for some variety in your diet. It is unsurprising, then, that when Clarke aided Selvon through his rough transition into Canadian literature, he sought to help Selvon find "the quickest way . . . to make some easy and fairly good bread, to help [him] buy a piece of salt fish and a roti" (October 21, 1977). Similarly, they recognized that it was not just a matter of getting good bread; it was also about who you can or cannot break bread with. To Selvon, Clarke's reputation preceded him: "I hear you have five-six mansions in various parts of Canada, and you does invite the Mayor of Toronto for pigtail and rice" (November 9, 1976). Such facetious remarks were standard in the banter between two writers known for their humour. As with their fiction, however, their laughter responded to real social pressures that threatened to erode their dignity. These lighthearted comments about whose bread may be buttered were made alongside genuine concern for each other's ability to be breadwinners.

Their exchanges of advice sought a balance between financial stability and professional integrity. On the one hand, they were contemplating the desperation of Selvon's early years in Calgary. While Clarke served as an important point of contact in Toronto, Selvon initially found few rewarding opportunities in Calgary and in this time of limited choices, he became a janitor at the University of Calgary, where he was later to become writer-in-residence. His mounting frustration during this period took the form of his semi-serious complaint that he "can't even buy mouth-organ for [his] son for Christmas, nor boil a ham" (December 6, 1980). On the other hand, both Clarke and Selvon knew that for racialized writers such as themselves, even when bread is hard to come by, they had to remain wary of underselling their work. On February 24, 1981, Clarke defiantly stated, "If we let them pay we small potatoes, they will consider our work to be small potatoes. Let me go bankrupt and keep my fucking integrity. Suck salt be-Jesus-Christ, and drink water to keep my belly full." They intended to refuse crumbs from a white literary establishment they knew from experience was prone to belittling the contributions of Black and East Indian writers.

In striving to keep each other's pantry full, however, Clarke and Selvon were not disinterested parties. The bountiful spread they expected whenever they visited one another was literal, and the specifics were a regular point of debate. After securing a few profitable opportunities in the first few months of 1982, Selvon, feeling his oats so to speak, warned, "You'll have to do better than stale B.C. salmon and Hudson Bay, though; it is Chivas Regal and Dublin Bay scampi or nothing at all" (April 6, 1982). Their letters especially belaboured these anticipated and promised meals, not only because of the Caribbean brand of hospitality previously mentioned, but because of a sub-par meal served in the early days of their friendship that Selvon never let Clarke forget. Clarke explains the circumstances and contents of this meal in *A Passage Back Home*. Hurriedly prepared because of the unexpected nature of the visit, this meal, Clarke grudgingly admits, comprised "food [that] was either frozen or else not in adequate portions." While hardly a significant fault to many of their readers, Selvon stood ready to niggle Clarke when announcing upcoming visits: "I don't want no stale pork chops what leftover from last night, nor any of that evil Hudson Bay whiskey!" (July 4, 1980). The camaraderie between these two men is apparent, but their culinary references were also opportunities for them to display their poise as writers. On December 16, 1985, Clarke wrote to Selvon, "Whilst you having ham: I having salt fish; whilst you having black pudding and souse: I having a biscuit and a piece o' hard chaddar; whilst you having drink; I having a beer; and whilst you mekking money 'pon race horse, I going be pelting some blows in this typewriter." Selvon was also ready with rhetorical bravado, as seen in a letter dated September 19, 1985 in which Selvon compared Clarke's planned trip to New Brunswick to his own trip to Trinidad: "Cold going to make your totee shrivel up and the foreskin would curl inwards and you can't find it when you want to pee. Mines would be bathed by tropical seawater and stimulated with canejuice and rum, and if I drink a fish-broth, I would not be responsible for the havoc it would cause." Their epistolary humour entertains, but as with their fiction, clever intersections of race, class, gender, and nationality can be teased out. Clarke jokingly juxtaposes the clichéd image of the starving artist diligently pursuing grand literary ambitions with the Caribbeanized man of leisure. Likewise, Selvon caricatures the tropical island that is ready to rejuvenate every tourist and that offers the ideal stimulants to heighten (and satisfy) male virility. They make fun of these images while acknowledging the real differences between writers with and without rewarding opportunities, as well as the nostalgia and desires of Caribbean immigrants.

A comparable sentiment emerges on February 27, 1979 as Clarke harangues Salkey: "a little bird told me, while I was in Brooklyn sleeping on the floor in my mother's slum house, that you were on the Riviera of luxury, sipping champagne and eating frogs' legs. I was eating Aunt Jemima pancakes with no syrup on them." These are fictional scenarios that highlight and mock real class differences. Clarke, however, cannot keep up the lie of being underfed while visiting his mother: "But really, Handrew, while I was in Brooklyn for two weeks, I ate more black pudding and souse, more fried chicken, more peas and rice, and drank more liquor than in all the days in Barbados, when foodstuffs were all-a-penny. I can't understand why you Yankees eat so much food." Passages like this one are precursors to Clarke's *Pig Tails* in that they anticipate Clarke's use of the figure of the mother "as the necessary catalyst who facilitates an engagement with the self as it confronts and accommodates its exilic disposition" (Mehta 324). Clarke underlines his imposition of an American identity on Salkey because of his cognizance of Salkey's discomfort with and in the American identity.

Clarke's characteristic interrogation of cross-cultural encounters can also be found intermingled with his discussion of food in his letters. On February 24, 1987, Clarke explains how his romantic relationship with an English woman is affecting his diet: "I now, in my fucking ante-old age, liking roast beef and Yorkshire pudding, like if um is a black pudding and cou-cou. Why you was silent 'pon these virtues o' the cullinerry harts?" He offers an extended discussion of what he calls "the transculturalization of my psyche," exclaiming at his change from a man "accustom to rackling-'bout ice in my glass, brack-ka-dakka-dak" to being "like kiss-me-arse Hinglish man, drinking scotch with water, and no fucking hice in the crystal glass!" Finally, he explains, "Man, you don't know that this woman now buying pig tail; hokra! ground nuts; sweet potato—not yams, man!—real sweet potato; heddoe; eating cou-cou and salt fish, with a butter-sauce, like if England had sugar plantation, and not cotton jennies." In typical Clarke fashion, his linguistic flourishes overflow with irony. He takes the kernel of truth that cultural exchange at the culinary level can be real and useful and exaggerates it to show how it can easily be misconstrued and romanticized.

What is clear from these letters is that Clarke was prone to rhapsodizing about food in a seemingly effortless and joyful manner. His detailing to Salkey of the menu for a dinner party he hosted comes across as proud, generous, and inviting: "And on Saturday, Greville Clarke's birthday, I hosted a dinner party for him. We had split-peas soup, each soup plate decorated with a juicy hunk of pig tail; roast joint of lamb, with potatoes, asparagus and rice with the stalks of beets" (April 6, 1987). His conjuring, again to Salkey, of a wished-for meal were it not for the responsibilities of that day's writing seems as satiating as the meal itself: "I feel peckish for a nice pudding and souse, a bowl o' jug-jug, some increase-peas and rice, with the rice grain hardish, a roast pork with the onion, the parsley, the thyme, the clove, and the garlin juck-in the pork, and um baking slow-slow, 'pon a low heat . . . with that, yuh have yuh lettuce, yuh spring tomatoes, yuh hard-boil eggs, and yuh avocado pear, with a sprinkling o' blue cheese 'pon top of it, a nice slice o' Wessindian sweet potato, and a bottle o' Chateauneuf de Pape" (Easter 1987). When fitted into Clarke's oeuvre, these riffs are emblematic of food's significance in both the political and literary histories of the Caribbean. These writers expand and remould the culinary discourse they inherited to discuss serious and unserious matters, generating mutual sustenance.

Notes

1 In a previous article, "Archived Relationships," I described Clarke's selling of his personal documents to a university as a "strategic, self-reflective collaboration" and examined the racialized macho performativity evident in those letters (178).

2 People's National Movement, Trinidad and Tobago's oldest and most dominant political party.

CHAPTER 10

Let Me Stand Up

Austin Clarke

This poem has Clarke grappling with one the central themes of his later writing: aging. The struggle against racism and the seemingly relentless procession of police violence and white indifference are all recast here as an exhausting burden for an aging man to contend with. The poet longs for a future in which he might slip into the night unremarked upon and merely walk the "criminal night" with nothing more than a "literary thought on my arm." This poem is undated but, based on the letterhead and format of the original, is likely from the early 1980s.

Let me be able to stand up, old,
When I'm past standing up
In youth: when age has bent
Me rusty, a hairpin superfluous
As neglect; when bed and toilet
Sleeping and waking, fade
Into one long television afternoon
Of snowflakes and of screams;
When I can walk the streets
With a simple stick for walking,
Not for knocking necessary heads,
When I can put the pen down, late
In the criminal night, and walk
With a literary thought on my arm,

And have no taxis stop, nor cop cars
Pause to see who the hell is out
So black, so late in this mumbling walk
With a woman in his thought
Walking arm on mind, with me
In the early fornicating hours
Of broken husbands and homeward lovers
Loveless, as four-legged garbagemen
Their heads downward in a sniffing prayer.
Let me be able to pause, if need be,
On the weight of my years, aimless
On a shiny washed and recent side street
Without one bead of anticipated fear
For the assaulting bouquet of a cop;
Without the needless need to hurry
Anywhere, when all my age demands
Is a short pause on its heavy stick.

CHAPTER 11

Austin A.C. Clarke Is the Most

Kate Siklosi

While poring over some of Clarke's early poetic manuscripts—
which are heavily revised, and bear the night scars of slashes,
rhetorical questions, and remedied inaccuracies—I came across
something seemingly rare in Clarke's literary and personal
oeuvre: an inward, romantic communing with nature at his
casement's ledge. While most of the more current writing and
scholarship on Clarke's work focuses, rightly so, on the exterior
worlds he imagined, lamented, and celebrated within the city of
Toronto, his early poetry betrays a sense of interiority and a yearning identification with the natural world. A lot of Clarke's political
writing throughout his career lingers on the boundary between
the exterior world, the interior spaces of his characters' minds,
and the domestic spaces they inhabit; in these early poems, we
see him experimenting with the thresholds of these borders. In
his meditations on the natural world outside his window, he is
writing through the co-production of identity between inside/
outside, and undoing such binaries—as the city moves, breathes,
and seethes, so the mind of the poet acts in response.

I came across two undated, handwritten poems—an "original," and then the revised and rewritten version, both written
in Clarke's characteristic sprawling calligraphy—reminiscent of
the dance of an ink-dipped spider drunk with elegant intent. The
first poem I assume to be the first draft, since its form is much

more tentative upon the page: it lacks the formal tightness and structure of the second, and the second has airs of Clarke painstakingly ruminating over the "right" descriptors, searching for the "proper" perspective to cloak the poem's intent. The poems are left undated, but based on their placing in Clarke's archives (and the fact that the second poem is written on University of Toronto letterhead), these poems were likely written in 1958 and 1959, while Clarke was a student at Trinity College.

As a young writer cutting his teeth as a poet, this mode also could be a means for Clarke to learn the craft he would, unfortunately, abandon for most of his career. Although his revisions are mostly to alter the meaning of the words themselves—"uncurtained birds and squirrels" in the first version becomes "unwarmed birds and squirrels" in the second—Clarke is also ever so slightly experimenting with form in these early poems.

The first draft is ten lines long, with lines one to four, seven, and ten written in a form roughly resembling iambic decapentasyllable, a Byzantine metre also known as "political verse." Political verse is known for the rhythmic movement created by its metre. When Clarke rewrote the poem, he split up some of the lines so that the "new" poem is twelve lines of varying lengths (roughly, longer lines followed by shorter ones) arranged in non-rhyming couplets with the second lines dropped or indented from the left margin. But the movement inherent in the political verse form is retained in this updated draft; the imagery and rhythm of the pastoral scene of "birds and squirrels / Living on the impulse of hardhearted loves, / in trees, and nests of everlasting lease," carries a musicality that suggests human connection and communion with nature. Early in his career, Clarke was introduced to the Romantic poets and the modernist T.S. Eliot. One of his earliest pieces of juvenile poetry, "We Are the Half-Born Men," is an obvious play on Eliot's infamous "The Hollow Men," a poem about hopeless immobility. Judging by Clarke's struggle to articulate natural worlds, both interior and exterior, across an axis of influence, it is plausible that he is experimenting with form using these writers as guides, their work serving as *Baedekers* with which he can imprint his own understanding of selfhood and interiority onto the world.

Political verse, or *politikos stichos*—"the verse of the polis and its citizens"—was also used as a poetic "form of the people" in the Byzantine Empire during the thirteenth century. I'm not suggesting here that Clarke was aware that he was writing in political verse form, or was even aware of it, but I found the resemblance, coupled with Clarke's literary polemic of engagement with the city and with citizenship, to be striking. Moreover, given Clarke's classical education and his literary apprenticeship with poet and editor Frank Collymore, founder of the Bajan literary magazine *Bim*, it seems plausible that Clarke could be adapting this classical form in his work, or at least might have been aware of it.

In its traditional use, political verse is not meant to imply a political tone or polemic, per se, but it was used as a secular form in medieval and modern Greek poetry. In Clarke's poems, we do not see a transcendental attribution of feeling to faith, but rather an exposition on the writing process itself as a secular practice. Although "the city" is mediated in these early Clarke poems through a landscape that does not signify as overly urban—he describes the view as more pastoral, with birds, squirrels, trees, and nests—the concerns of the outside world are latent, and they foreshadow the urban themes that would preoccupy most of his writing. In the first version of the poem, the opening line reads, "When the dawn of day props by the ledge," and this line is revised in the second version as "When the dawn of fear should prop / by the ledge." This revision of "day" to "fear" signals a foreboding sense of anticipated threat that emanates from the outside world, infiltrating the window of Clarke's house and soul.

Moreover, it is this inciting moment wherein the exterior world enters the poet's mind that initiates a process of metapoetic discovery in the remainder of the poems. The day's summoning, punctuated by the careless and carefree existence of the flora and fauna, leads him to reflect upon his own "grievances and pains," articulated through his "unapprenticed hand." The poems thus unfold a complex psychic landscape through the writing process, one that is mottled with self-discovery and self-doubt. As he meditates on the world outside his window and writes, the perfect and "everlasting lease" of the natural world's "beauty" and "truth" remind him of the perceived "unappropriateness" of his "mould." This perceived inadequacy could signify the poetic apprentice's self-doubt, or it could be Clarke ruminating on the inability of language to accurately describe beauty or truth—that it is an inherently flawed medium that can only gesture toward eternality and truth, hopelessly.

The ledge, however, becomes a psychic barrier; the dawn of day/fear "props by the ledge," meaning it does not necessarily cross the threshold of the window but tickles its boundary. In this way, Clarke signals an interiority that resists the imposing structures and ideas of the outside world; the window, then, becomes a significant site of potential resistance and psychic/physical protection from outside forces. Speaking of the window as a threshold, Clarke writes in the third line of the first version, "Separating and segregating me from a lower order." He then alters the line to "Separating, segregating me from reality on the second floor." This is an interesting revision, for in both he is playing on "separation" and "segregation" as racially loaded terms, and in the first he aligns his inability to articulate the essence of beauty and truth in nature as indicative of his "lower order." However, in the second version, the lower order becomes the safe haven of the second floor of his house—the site, presumably, from which he sits at his window ledge. Moving from an exterior, social reality—his racialized body as "lower order"—to a protective, domestic space signals the house as a threshold to the outside, but also as a haven that protects him, and allows him to trespass (if only in and through the moment of writing) the boundaries and structures of the outside world.

Thus, although these poems are not directly concerned with physical movement, in their rhythmic structure, and in their play with the window or "doorway," to borrow Dionne Brand's term, between inside and outside, they perform an incredible thought movement. It is significant that movement was a central concern of Clarke's throughout his writing career. Movement toward, movement from, movement between—these are means by which language can mobilize our particular imaginaries. Bodily movement, but also thought movement, becomes both an aesthetic and political act, especially in the context of the city, wherein the social structures are deeply racialized. In writing about the dreams of colonial subjects as narratives of possibility, Frantz Fanon, in *Black Skin, White Masks*, argues that these "are muscular dreams, dreams of action, dreams of aggressive vitality. I dream I am jumping, swimming, running, and climbing" (15). Movement, for Fanon, becomes a means by which the racialized body—whose movement is striated by exterior structures of control and containment—can imagine agency and possibility beyond the constraints of colonial order and its material structures. In Clarke's early poems, the city represents a space of unattainable and inimitable "beauty" and "truth," a space that he cannot attempt to recreate with his "unapprenticed hands, mis-shaped, mis-used / By careless scalpel and careering mind." He doesn't so much describe physical movement, but the psychic movement that takes place at the ledge of the window, the threshold between public and private.

At the window, Clarke articulates the Fanonian paradox of hope through the lens of the metapoetic process: he admires the animals outside the window for their natural freedom of movement, and yet his perceived inability to write accurately about his connection and communion with this outside world is conveyed with uncertainty and doubt, as if he is contained or restrained by his lack of ability to "make it cohere," as Pound says (Canto 116, 816). Again, this constraint could signify Clarke's revelling in the very inability of language, flowing through the vehicle of his hand, to accurately portray such truths he sees reflected in the outside world. Constraint, then, could be construed as a refusal to impose closure on meaning through writing, instead opting for an "everlasting lease" on that which we cannot know and can only imagine.

His hesitancy is perfectly marked by the line "Austin A C Clarke is the most," written below the first draft of the poem. I linger on this fragment. Is it an interrupted attempt to describe himself? A halted moment of confession, diary, self-questioning from an otherwise publicly proud man? Such questions make me uncomfortable, for working with the archives of a writer—especially when that writer has manuscripts written feverishly on napkins or coffee-stained foolscap with late-night meanderings noted in the marginalia—always seems like an act of trespassing. But the incompleteness of this sentence struck me, and I could not resist.

We see here a poet who is unconfident at least, and yet striving, poignantly, toward precision—a man experimenting with form and process, conveying his view of the transcendent connections between public and private worlds. It is the discordances and correspondences that surface in the metapoetic process—the struggles to define the world and the poet in it accurately on the page—that make the writing process part and parcel of a lived, practised reality integrated with dreams of moving potential, thresholds of desire as yet undone by exterior forces of containment and governance. Although he cannot replicate the truth and beauty of the outside world on the page, the very act of writing allows him to meet the city on the level of co-production and exchange. For Clarke, the natural world abides by a natural order that conveys its "truth"—as such, the poem becomes a space wherein the poet may gesture toward truth and knowledge, but the grand mystery of the world is forever left elusive. It is a poetics ruled not by the singular exactness of the facts, but the productive interchange between actors in an environment.

Clarke's window provides a view of the poet entering into a relationship of exchange and encounter with the outside world, but it's useful to think of the other window through which we encounter our world: language. In these early poems, we see Clarke experimenting with language, acutely aware of how slight turns in meaning can alter the axis and rotation of the poem as a whole. Language is a mediator between what is fixed and rigid and what is fluid and ungraspable. It is the window between structure and immensity, the pane against which we place our soul when we write. And whether or not we have the right words at the right time, the accurate thought and movement, is irrelevant. As Dionne Brand writes in *thirsty*, "Look it's like this, I'm just like the rest, / limping across the city, flying when I can" (57). Sitting at his window, painstakingly revising the form and content of his visions, the city—as seen and felt through the window—becomes a radical site of spiritual interaction and exchange. It is through Clarke's windows—architectural, corporeal, temporal—that we imagine and 'member the world.

N.B. These are my only copies.

When the dawn of fear should prop
     by the ledge in the ancient pile of cares
And blinks in half-sleep through last summer's
          clouded memories
Separating, segregating me from reality on the second floor
     of un-warmed birds and squirrels
Living on the impulse of hardhearted loves,
     in trees, and nests of everlasting lease,
Your grievances and pains, notches in of your mould
     in unapprenticed hands, mis-shaped, mis-used
By careless scalpel and careering mind
     unappropriate to beauty and to truth

One of Austin Clarke's earliest poems.
Permissions: William Ready Division of Archives and Research Collections, McMaster University Library

CHAPTER 12

The Rogue in Me

Austin Clarke

"The Rogue is Me" is one of Clarke's earliest recorded publications, dated 1956, the year after he moved from Barbados to Canada. While the poem is highly symbolist, it also demonstrates Clarke's classical training along-side his early adoption of modernist themes of decay, rebirth, and regeneration. The "grandfather's clocks / That keep dead time, time without a beat" contrast with the "roots of my tomorrows" and the "green fertilities of youth." "The Rogue in Me" was published in The Trinity Review, *the literary arts publication of Trinity College at the University of Toronto.*

In my brain are the rogue and the thief,
The thief that steals the sorrow and the blood from life;
In my brain are the nurse and the hangman's rope
That ties life with death, and death with hope.
In my blood is the surge of trees cut down in storms,
Of rivers muddy with floods of lives and tears,
With old women's bags, and grandfather's clocks
That keep dead time, time without a beat;
In my fears are the fears of Cleopatra,
Fears of death, fears for the dead.
I have lived one thousand years in tree and bush,
And have died with every fall of leaf,
And withered in each rainless season;

But deep down in the roots of my tomorrows
Are many fresh green fertilities of youth.
I, the tree without a branch, am climbing,
Climbing up toward heaven where lies no god,
No mercy, no hope for the hoping, no good
For the godly. The cliff and crags of my mind
Simmer in the nightly naked tormentation
Above earth's average human skyline . . .
Boats sail in my mind, in, and out again.
Boats without sails and spars, boats rudderless,
Like skeletons with the world's glory
Skimming through them examiningly.

CHAPTER 13

Spatiality in the Poetry of Austin A.C. Clarke

Stephen Cain[1]

To readers who primarily associate Austin Clarke with the writing of short fiction, memoirs, essays and award-winning novels, it must have come as some surprise to see him turn to the genre of poetry in the two late publications *Where the Sun Shines Best* (2013) and *In Your Crib* (2015). After all, poetry is typically viewed as a young person's activity—few writers take up poetry in their later years, and even those who have practised poetry throughout their careers rarely create significant verse in old age. Yet those who have followed Clarke's work closely will know that, in fact, he did begin his writing career by publishing verse—indeed, award-winning poetry, which I believe represents his very earliest Canadian publications—with five poems in *The Review* of Trinity College, in 1957. Moreover, thanks to the archival work of Paul Barrett, we now know that Clarke wrote poetry throughout his career and that the issues raised through his poetry resonate throughout his more public prose.

These many issues, ranging from police violence and the surveillance of Black communities in Canada, to the fears of old age and personal regrets, are all certainly worth investigating in his poetry, but what I wish to do in this chapter is to use his early poetry as a basis to examine his later verse, and to highlight two elements that seem to me to most strongly characterize his poetry: form (both generic and metric) and, more importantly, Clarke's attention to space and spatiality.

The significance of space is apparent in much of Clarke's verse, but is made overt in his frequent use of adverbs of place, demonstratives, and prepositions, most notably in the very titles of his two volumes of poetry: *WHERE the Sun Shines Best*, and *IN your Crib*. But we see this attention to space even in the earliest verse of the 1950s. For example, in the second of two Trinity College poems[2] reprinted in *The Austin Clarke Reader* (henceforth *ACR*), "From My Lover's Home," a lyrical lament regarding the absence of the loved one is represented in explicitly spatial terms: "From my lover's home to me there is the sea" (*ACR* 254). However, this is not a topographic poem describing a landscape and state of mind, but rather one in which the poetic speaker's body is imbricated; as he later writes: "There is the sea from my lover's home and me. / Right down my side, right down my left side / There is the sea, the dark sea" (254).

In contrast, with regard to the earlier Trinity College poem, "Fishermen Looking Out to Sea," we do see a more externalized, topographic gaze at work, with a disembodied speaker gazing at fishermen, who in turn, look outside the poetic frame to the sea. An elegy, rather than a lover's lament, for the deaths of generations of fishermen and a premonition of the subject's future death by drowning, the poem is marked by the repeated refrain, "Why do you sit beneath the burning August sun"? (253–54).

I mention the presence of a refrain, for this poem is much more formally complex than "From My Lover's Home"; so complex and obscure, in fact, that many readers would likely require recourse to poetic guidebooks to recognize that the poem closely resembles the medieval French form known as the *rondeau redoublé*. The *rondeau* itself is a rather arcane form, especially in English, but the *rondeau redoublé* is even rarer, consisting as it does of five quatrains and a quintet with refrains repeated on lines 1–4, and then on lines 8, 12, 16, 20, and 25.[3] An uncommon form, and certainly not often practised in the twentieth century, one of the few English medieval poets who explored the *rondeau* (or *rondel/roundel*) was Chaucer. Clarke's experimentation with this form indicates the strong influence exerted on his work by the traditional English canon, and his school-days reading of Chaucer is noted at length in the sixteenth chapter of his memoir *'Membering*, where Clarke recalls studying Chaucer in 1953 and using the language and style of *The Canterbury Tales* to write texts that describe his classmates' "oddities." In retrospect, he sees these works as his first attempts at poetry: "These character sketches were my first ramblings into creative writing. I enjoyed writing these capsules of character; and I became good at them; and they made the literary maga- zine which we edited and published, in the long tradition of Sixth Form boys editing college magazines" (247–48). Whether Charles Chadwick, the editor at *The Review* and judge of the poetry con- test for 1957, was more impressed by Clarke's complex prosody or the poem's uncommon imagery, "Fishermen Looking Out to Sea" nonetheless became Clarke's first literary success, garnering him a cash prize of five dollars (Algoo-Baksh 37).

In her 1994 biography of Clarke, Stella Algoo-Baksh notes that after winning the poetry award in *The Review,* "Clarke wrote other poems and offered them to Chadwick, but while the latter provided critiques, advice, and support he did not think Clarke's new work merited publication" (37). However, Clarke did in fact publish two more poems with *The Review* in the following issue (not indi- cated by Algoo-Baksh or included in her bibliography of Clarke's periodical publications), again writing as A.A. Chesterfield-Clarke. Both poems reveal Clarke's traditional English influences,[4] in this case the Romanticism of Keats, but with an E.A. Poe flavour, as in lines from "The Rogue in Me": "In my fears are the fears of Cleopatra, / Fears of death, fears for the dead. / I have lived one thousand years in trees and bush, / And have died with every fall of leaf, / And withered with each rainless season" (13). The second poem in that issue, "He Walks Beside the Sea," however, now adds perambulation to Clarke's established preference for a poetics of static space: "He walks beside the sea, a trifling profile

/ Mistakenly created. / He walks by the sea, on a cross of sorrows" (33). While somewhat overwrought in its affect, this poem does, however, mark a change from the more imagistic use of landscape in his previous poems to a new interest in combining emotion with spatiality that will become more pronounced in future works.

Clarke's first post-university publications were two poems in the short-lived Toronto little literary magazine *Evidence* (ten issues, 1960–67, edited by Kenneth Craig). While the second of these poems, "Kirkland, North by North," which appeared in issue 2 of *Evidence*, is mentioned by Algoo-Baksh in her biography, the first untitled poem, which appeared in the previous issue, is not, nor is it listed her in bibliography of Clarke's publications. This four-page poem is, however, discussed at some length by Clarke in *'Membering*, in which he characterizes it as overly influenced by "T.S. Eliot in some of the music and phrasing, and Dylan Thomas's echoes in the other lines. It is obvious to me, fifty-two years after this was first published, what I was reading, either for pleasure, or for instruction" (351).

Indeed, the Thomas elements are quite pronounced in the poem, with strong echoes of the pastoral "Fern Hill," such as:

> In my barefoot days, under the sun, blackened
> By miles of walking, and moons of coming, and never going,
> In my bastard days, young and pure; before
> I saw everything, but innocence in girls,
> Browned and cocoed, on beaches, marbly
> Under the sore foot, and lazy as my native-cousins
> Stretching in yawns till moonshine come. . . .
> Through the track and gully, through the backyard
> Of the Bishop's, strangled with sacred linen
> On the sycamore tree, all brambles and no leaves
> That wagged its mouth over the Hill. (n.p.)

Beyond its value in indicating Clarke's early influences, this poem also demonstrates his poetic development from the Trinity College poems, both in its length and its attention to space. Once again we see the emphasis on prepositions ("under the sun," "on beaches," "under the sore foot," "through the track and gully, through the backyard," "on the sycamore," "over the Hill"), but what is added in this poem is a more resonant subjectivity, with the poet moving from the use of a generic "he" to a detailed, seemingly autobiographical sketch of a youth spent in Barbados.

"Kirkland, North by North," the second of the *Evidence* poems, is a page longer, but even more wide-ranging in its perspectives.[5] Likely inspired by Clarke's experience as a newspaper reporter working in Timmins and Kirkland Lake from Christmas 1959 to the winter of 1961 (Algoo-Baksh 42–43), this poem is ambitious in its geographic invocation and anticipates Clarke's use of space to structure a sustained narrative that he will master in *Where the Sun Shines Best*. In what has at this point become a characteristic move, Clarke's poem begins with a poetic gaze at a fixed landscape:

> Here lies tons of driftwood under snow
> Summer lakes and winter-rinks
> With their fingers twixt the page
> Of their thoughts of snow and drink. (n.p.)

However, after five quatrains of description of a snowbound mining town, the poem shifts both formally and subjectively to consider the life of an unfulfilled woman in the North whose life is compared metaphorically to a dry well:

> Thirty times, in years, has her rope and pail
> Touched bottom and come up unadorned
> With rope, and pail, and moss: come waterless,
> And she had waited at the top, expectant with dried lips
> To kiss the drops of any liquid thing:
> Water or growth, or well or love. (n.p.)

What unites the first section of the poem to this seemingly incongruous moment, however, is the repeated image of snow. As he writes earlier of the woman: "Thirty years have stretched before her like a road / A road in winter, long, and empty like a winter road. / And snow, her only sure companion which always came" (n.p.). Indeed, just as snow is referenced twice in the first stanza of the poem, it continues to appear throughout the second section, and ultimately connects to the third movement of the poem, which describes the main street of Kirkland Lake:

> A man living in the North thinks nothing
> But snow; sees nothing but snow; is nothing
> But snow, and abomination. (n.p.)

Acting almost as a refrain at this point, the invocation of snow then allows the poet to observe and comment upon various citizens of the town moving along the icy main street, such as the alcoholic Old John, the sex worker Celeste, and a mysterious, unnamed man who walks the street cloaked in a fur coat and whose thoughts then conclude the poem:

> A man making his home in God's north country
> Cannot afford to think of God
> The snow is too omnipotent. (n.p.)

With "Kirkland, North by North," then, we can observe Clarke moving from his earlier poems representing fixed landscapes and singular perspectives to a new, more wide-ranging eye, taking in several spaces and subjectivities. The use of snow, both as meteorological and geographical phenomenon (as it falls, as it settles and changes the terrain of the town), and as an element that the various citizens experience and share, is an innovative way of structuring a long poem, one to which Clarke will return in *Where the Sun Shines Best*, where he uses the space of Moss Park, but also its fallen leaves and environmental conditions, to connect and examine the lives of both the homeless and the military recruits at the armoury.

In her contribution to this volume ("Austin A.C. Clarke Is the Most"), Kate Siklosi discusses a final poem from this early 1950–60

period. Siklosi describes this text as a type of pastoral where the
poetic speaker situates themselves at a "second floor" window
ledge contemplating the natural world of "unwarmed birds and
squirrels / living . . . in trees." What is striking to me about this
short early poem, however, is how it immediately establishes
the spatial position of his poetic speaker—a tendency extended
across his two last two book-length poems—as an observer at a
second-floor window gazing at park-like space.

While Siklosi's admirably perceptive reading notes that
Clarke's form may be a "Byzantine metre also known as 'political
verse,'" she is also careful to indicate that this does not "imply
a political tone or polemic, per se." Yet the political edge of
Clarke's poetics does become more pronounced in his poetry of
the 1980s. Thinking of politics in this later poetry, I am reminded
of a quotation from Clarke's 1992 essay "Public Enemies: Police
Violence and Black Youth," wherein he writes that when faced
with injustice, and angry, he turns to poetry: "I am part of that
anger. I am aware of the despair. I am part of that despair. The
rage is mine. But I, armed with greater age (if not greater wisdom
as a consequence), put my reliance on the poets" (343). Certainly
we can see, with respect to his two known poems from the 1980s,
a new turn to anger and politics on Clarke's part.

"Do Not Let Them Choose the Fragrance," published in
this collection, addresses the 1979 murder of Albert Johnson by
Toronto police, and since it does not directly involve spatiality
or poetic form, I will not discuss it at length, but will merely note
how it anticipates two issues that he will explore in his last two
poetry collections. First, by dedicating the poem to Johnson's
widow and the mother of his children, "Mrs. Lemona Johnson,"
Clarke stresses the importance of the presence of the Black maternal, which will be discussed at the climax of *Where the Sun Shines
Best*; and second, by addressing his poem to—by directly speaking to and giving guidance to—Johnson's children, Clarke makes
an early foray into examining the role elder poetic speakers can
play in advising a younger Black generation, which he will do at
greater length in *In Your Crib*.

The second 1980s poem, also published here and entitled "Let Me Stand Up," invokes space and race in a direct way. Clarke's poem expresses a desire, or an imperative demand, to feel free to walk the city streets at night without fear, which he hopes to do in his old age, as he cannot do now:

> Let me be able to stand up, old,
> When I'm past standing up
> In youth: when age has bent
> Me rusty, a hairpin superfluous
> As neglect. . . .
> When I can walk the streets
> With a simple stick for walking,
> Not for knocking necessary heads,
> When I can put the pen down, late
> In the criminal night, and walk
> With a literary thought on my arm (n.p.)

This desire to walk at night, expressed in poetic terms, invokes the French Symbolist tradition of the flâneur—that late nineteenth-century poetic speaker exemplified by Charles Baudelaire, who wanders the streets freely in the late-night and pre-dawn hours making poetic observations on the marginal—the late-night drinkers, the working classes ending or beginning a shift, the criminals, the homeless, the sex workers. So these subsequent lines by Clarke, with the speaker "So black, so late in this mumbling walk / With a woman in his thought / Walking arm on mind, with me / In the early fornicating hours / Of broken husbands and homeward lovers / Loveless, as four-legged garbagemen / Their heads downward in a sniffing prayer" (n.p.) should awaken in the reader a recognition of Baudelairean imagery and subject matter.

Yet key to the flâneur's mobility in space and place is his invisibility: the Baudelairean flâneur moves unobserved and unnoticed himself as only a white bourgeois citizen of Paris can. In the case of Clarke, as a Black flâneur, he reflects that he cannot go out at night and not be noticed, and in fact must always fear the

"the assaulting bouquet of a cop" (n.p.). At this point in Canadian history, Clarke claims there is no space for a Black flâneur; the Black body is under constant observation and threatened by state violence. The poem is thus an indictment of the present society, and a wish for a future time when—either because he is old, and thereby not seen as a threat to the enforcers of a white metropolis, or because the inherent racism of that society has abated—Black subjects are free to walk unmolested, and unnoted, at night.

Thirty years later, that freedom has failed to arise; and while the poetic speaker of Clarke's long poem *Where the Sun Shines Best* does remark that he infrequently walks through the used condoms, cigarette butts, and other detritus of Moss Park during the day, he is now more often than not restricted to a single space—a second-floor window of his apartment. Despite this lack of mobility, the poet's view, and indeed the entirety of the poem, is still structured through place and space, in this case Moss Park and its environs: its armoury, hockey arena, playground, baseball diamond, Salvation Army shelters, and three cathedrals. We see this emphasis on space, particularly as a site of struggle, in the very opening stanza:

> THE YELLOW leaves are trampled over by the black
> boots of three soldiers from the Moss Park Armouries;
> in uniform, intended not to be seen, nor identified,
> for their intention and profession is to kill. . . .
> War. War has been declared.
> War. It is all that's on their minds. War;
> and the intention for war declared upon Moss Park. (7)

One might also consider that this attention to space is given to the reader paratextually, even before s/he reads the first few lines of the poem, as the cover image of the book, which depicts a park bench with a grove of trees behind and a pool of blood in the foreground, emphasizes that place is paramount, and the interior pages of the book are also "watermarked" with an image of a park bench and dead leaves and debris.

The unfolding of Clarke's poetic re-imaging of the 2005 murder of Paul Croutch, a homeless man and former newspaper editor, by three Canadian reservists, one of whom was not white, is primarily spatial. That is, as the poet-speaker watches from his second-storey window across the street to the park, various figures enter his line of sight, which then prompts poetic responses and examination of that subject: for example, a group of Muslim women pushing baby strollers prompts a meditation upon family structures, questions of paternity and maternity, Islamophobia, and Canada's involvement in the war in Afghanistan. Most often, however, it is a trio of homeless men of different races who walk across the park toward the poet's window over a series of three mornings that allows the poet to meditate upon poverty, addiction, immigration, and racism. More significantly, their walk parallels the movements of the three soldiers, which then causes the poet to imagine the murder for which they are responsible.

I find this a very innovative way of structuring a long poem—the sixty-three discrete stanzas are not linked by time or linear narrative (for example, the murder of the homeless man is imagined at the beginning, middle, and end of the poem); nor necessarily by theme (one stanza discussing militarism is not necessarily followed by another extending that idea, but can switch to, say, a discussion of betting on horses at Woodbine); nor are they structured purely by memory and associative stream of thought, but by space.

But strangely, in a poem interested in space and place, the title of which points to the question of place, "where the sun shines best" is not upon a place, but—puzzlingly and problematically—upon a person, or image of a person. That is, many readers will recognize "where the sun shines best" as a line from the racist minstrel song "My Mammy."

My first reaction to the inclusion of this racist lyric is that Clarke is pointing out a false consciousness or false identification; just as the Black soldier, by enlisting, falsely allies himself with white imperialism, and by standing by while a marginalized subject is murdered, with classist militarism, so is Clarke's evocation of a racist lyric an example of how popular culture interpolates Black subjects to identify with racist images. Maggie Quirt, however, in her review of *Where the Sun Shines Best*, argues that Clarke's inclusion of this problematic lyric is thematically important to the poem as a whole as a moment of shared marginality on the part of the characters in the poem, and of resistance to multiple forms of oppression. Noting that the most popular rendition of "My Mammy" is by Al Jolson, "himself the victim of anti-Semitism and a proponent of equal rights for all" (391), Quirt suggests that by referencing Jolson and this song Clarke "makes connections between oppressed communities across space and time, teasing out alliances and postulating bridges to bring us closer to, not away from, understanding" (390).

Indeed, Clarke does directly state that the image of the mammy, even if voiced through blackface, is of value:

MAMMY-MAMMY-Mammy! Take this plea of love
and blood even from the reddened lips in a face
of black shoe polish, recite the confidence in his minstrel (66)

But more than a general call for understanding, as Quirt suggests, I read Clarke's gesture here as invoking the image of the empathetic and suffering Black maternal as a palliative against the cruelty, racism, class division, hatred, and militarism of the men described in the poem. Moreover, it should also be noted that Clarke dedicates the entirety of the poem to a maternal figure—"For Gladys Irene Jordan Clarke-Luke, My Mother. 1914–2005"—which suggests the image and redemptive power of the maternal may be the central theme of the poem.

Yet immediately preceding, and following, this passage, a maternal figure (a homeless woman who calls 911 for help during the murder) is also assaulted by the soldiers, with Clarke stating, "we have killed the woman into silence" (69). The poem then ends with an invective against the Black soldier, who will be left alone:

fumbling with the cord knotted
round truth and stupidity and loyalty, thick as the dust
you will breathe in Kandahar, if you get there still, to carry
out the killing ordered by war, and patriotism (70)

Turning from the failure, or repression, of the Black maternal, we might then see Clarke's last book, *In Your Crib*, as an attempt at responding to social injustice through the Black paternal. The poem is doubly addressed, with an elder male speaker attempting to provide advice to a young Black man in his neighbourhood. We see this double articulation even in the title: if we take "crib" first as vernacular for house or apartment, "in your crib" describes the spatial position of the poem (what the poet thinks about in his house), but "crib" can be taken allegorically to address the young man, who the poet sees as immature—that is, someone failing to leave the crib, as in cradle or playpen.

But the poem is not only spatialized by its title; like *Where the Sun Shines Best*, the poem is structured by place and by figures who enter the poet's personal space. Still seated at the second-floor window, the poet's line of sight seems to have diminished, as he now no longer looks across the park to the playgrounds and benches, but only to the sidewalk and street immediately in front of him. The poem begins with the image of motion through space which is immediately abetted—the inaugural moment of the poem is a car accident outside the speaker's home where the young man's vehicle crashes:

The Mercedes-Benz,
statue of wealth and beauty and geometric design:
an inverted Y? An M? Fresh
from a carwash, in this neighbourhood,
with high-powered soap sprays
like those from a gun . . . you know guns.
And how fast they can travel; faster than the Benz
in third shifting gear. Bram! The grill smashed dead.
Crumpled in water-melon fragility. (*In Your Crib* 2)

The poem then unfolds with the poet contemplating the appearance and attitude of the young man, watching as he is interrogated by the police. This scene, of a young Black man driving a car being stopped by the police, recurs throughout Clarke's oeuvre, yet here the poet is positioned at a remove from the incident. Then, in turn, the poet begins to question himself and how he has failed to help this young man at that moment, and through his past actions.

Generically and formally, *In Your Crib* is much more polyphonic and fluid than *Where the Sun Shines Best*. In the latter poem, the metre is most often iambic septameter, the long lines suggesting formal meditation and political importance. With *In Your Crib*, however, Clarke makes full use of varied metrics and lineation—many short lines and single words in white space recalls the jazz-influenced poetry of mid-period Amiri Baraka, and even directly quotes Baraka's "Black Art" (44). While Steven W. Beattie misidentifies the free verse in this poem as "blank verse" in his *Quill and Quire* review of *In Your Crib*, he rightly connects Clarke's prosody here to jazz and reggae: "the poet's own influences run more to Coltrane and the reggae of Bob Marley. The latter's 'Redemption Song' looms large over this book, as it did in 'Old Pirates, Yes, They Rob I,' from the author's 2013 story collection, *They Never Told Me*" (33). Indeed, just as Clarke has used the refrain in several of his earlier poems, the lyrics of Marley's anthem often function as such here. The poem also moves through various tonal registers and genres, ranging from the didactic, to the invective, to the sermon, to the elegy, and finally, as Clarke begins to quote from his own past works (lines like "when he was free and young and he used to wear silks" and "there are no elders" being the titles of previous story collections), the poem seems to become an assessment of Clarke's own life and writing career, and in some sense he appears to pen his own poetic eulogy.

That is, after critiquing the young man for his style of dress, his language, his musical taste, his lack of community involvement, the elder poet then turns to his own failings as an activist, a leader, a parent, as a general father figure—and eventually comes to a point of acceptance of both himself and the young man: rap after all, can be considered a form of poetry, and is similar to the blues; the young man's confidence and toughness is a requirement for survival; and community still exists. The poem then ends, not with advice and instruction, but with a blessing:

> Look up; send your glance to the apex of the limbs;
> and see the silent declaration in the swifted-up expulsion:
> the children of the maples, as you count
> the days in your life, will pass through
> before summer and light, and love, and you shall walk
> on the same threading buds and flowers . . .
> exclaiming in a new joy and wonder
> that you are now, living amongst neighbours
> who see only, the colour of your heart. (53)

Leslie Sanders, in her essay "Austin Clarke's Poetic Turn," observes that the last lines of *In Your Crib* appear to echo the thought of Martin Luther King, whom Clarke criticized earlier in his writing career: "the poem's conclusion is both stirring and somewhat ironic. Clarke's 1968 essay 'The Confessed Bewilderment of Martin Luther King and the Idea of Non Violence as a Political Tactic' is, as the title suggests, deeply critical of King. . . . Nevertheless the poem concludes with a not dissimilarly expressed hope" (74). Yet, at the same time, it is strangely appropriate for a poem—Clarke's last poem—in which old ideas, themes, images, and phrases are revisited and revised. Most striking to me is that once again, as in that very early untitled poem of the 1950s, we have the poet by a window, looking out, and pondering the distinction between his interior life and the external world. The reliance on a poetics of space and spatiality has remained consistent throughout Clarke's writing—from fisherman looking out to sea, to the snowscape of Kirkland Lake, to the flâneur walking at night, to the "battlefield" of Moss Park—but

what changes in this final poem is the prosody: whereas these earlier poems are written in a metre and style that emulated the writers of the white English canon (Chaucer, Eliot, Keats, Thomas),
in his last poem we now witness Clarke writing about civic and
societal issues in freer, more polyphonic language that incorpor-
ates the tone and rhythms of Baraka, of Marley, of Coltrane, but is
ultimately personal in style; not without its doubts, but nevertheless a powerful, public, and singular voice.

Notes

1   Thanks to Paul Barrett, Tim Conley, and Leslie Sanders for comments
    and suggestions on this chapter, as well as on an earlier version pre-
    sented at Austin Clarke's Legacy: A Celebration and Conference at
    York University in November 2017. That earlier version is scheduled to
    appear in a future issue of *TOPIA*.

2   Clarke, writing as A.A. Chesterfield-Clarke, published a series of
    poems in *The Review* of Trinity College, University of Toronto, in 1957
    under the general title "Five Poems From Barbados," which included
    "Fishermen Looking Out To Sea," "Do Not Come," "Three Years," "The
    Trees," and "From My Lover's Home." As only two of these poems are
    included in *The Austin Clarke Reader* (1996), I have assumed that these
    are the ones that Clarke considered his more mature poetic work of the
    time, and have therefore chosen to discuss them here.

3   Clarke's poem extends the final stanza to ten lines, rather than a quin-
    tet, and his refrains are taken from words in the first stanza, rather than
    the first complete line of the poem. Definition taken from Turco 1968.

4   In an interview with Camille A. Isaacs in 2013, when asked about his
    late-career return to poetry, Clarke responded: "I always thought that
    poetry was a trumpet played by clearer notes. I was brought up on Eliot,
    Keats, and Milton" (24).

5   Due to its ambiguous layout, a common characteristic of this type of
    small-press magazine, it is unclear whether "Kirkland, North by North"
    is a single long poem or a series of poems under that general title. The
    lineation and stanzaic structure suggest that it is three discrete poems
    dealing with the North, but without any section indicators, subtitles, or
    numbers to justify separation, I will consider this poem as a single unit.

CHAPTER 14

The Lessons of Austin Clarke

Sonnet L'Abbé

I met Austin Clarke in late 1996 at the University of Guelph, where he was that year's writer-in-residence. He didn't yet have the dreads I would later see him rocking at literary festivals. They had given him an office; two days a week he sat at a desk with his back to the window. I would show up for an appointment and he would wave me in without looking up from what he was doing. Often, he was writing a letter. He wrote in a broad, bold hand that looked to me to be literal calligraphy: he used a cartridge pen with a golden nib with a wide, flat edge against toothy paper. I would slide into the chair and sit there uncertainly, staring at this Real Writer, a product of the Caribbean encounter with British dipsy-doodling. As I waited, the room was silent except for the *scritch-scritch* of his pen, punctuated occasionally by a slightly longer *scrootch*, as, with a flourish, he'd put a tail on a "g" or a "y." It could be ten minutes before he was ready to give me his attention. And even once we started speaking, I could lose him: sometimes, in the middle of our meeting, he would decide he had to call Barry Callaghan. He'd bid me to stay put, pick up the phone, turn toward the window and talk for a squirmingly long time. Maybe he thought he was treating me to a private performance of the verbal bullshit artistry of old-school literary bros.

"Young L'Abbé," he said to me in one of those meetings, "these literary people are *racists!*" He said it like he was genuinely surprised that a long, unwillingly entertained suspicion had been confirmed. We were still a few years before *The Polished Hoe*. He had just won some other recognition, but seemed in that moment to be processing the fact that he *knew* the people who had given it to him. Austin had been hanging out all along with the people who would give him recognition, now or in the future, or who would withhold it, and he was not optimistic about their capacity to recognize Black excellence.

I showed Austin the fiction and poetry I was writing, telling him I didn't want to be a "Black writer," or a "brown writer," or "an immigrant's kid writer." I just wanted to be "a writer." He nodded. "You are just a writer," he said. "And you still are what you are." Like the other older, male mentors to whom I had read my work, he was uninterested in my stories exploring all the sexist microaggressions I had lived by the time I was twenty-two. My poems, however, seemed to hold his attention. He showed a few to Connie Rooke, and shortly thereafter one of my poems was accepted by the *Malahat Review*. I was floored.

Austin Clarke writing.
Permissions: William Ready Division of Archives and Research Collections, McMaster University Library

What Austin taught me was how much context mattered. I had sent my poems to the *Malahat* on my own, with a cover letter saying I'd had one piece in *Existère*, and had been rejected. Now, the same poems (as in, written by the same young person, with the same sensibility, during the same period), made it in, because the right person had introduced me. I had never gotten anything because I knew someone; I wanted merit to be everything. It would be years before I seriously questioned whether male mentors' estimations of my fiction had more to do with their estimations of my subject matter than my skill. Austin's help was, in a way, a lesson about Blackness, in the sense that I, too, would have to always negotiate a world where, talent or no, my career would depend heavily on relationships with white folks whose interest in non-white experience was beyond my control, yet who would have the biggest say in whether my work deserved to be published or rewarded.

Austin was working on *Pig Tails 'n Breadfruit* at the time. Over the fall term, he hosted regular soirées in the suite where he stayed on campus. Austin held court, teaching me and other young writers like Akinsola Jeje, Stephen Wicary, and Joanna Cockerline how to make a proper martini and how to drink quite a few of them. At one of these get-togethers, Austin spent most of the evening in the kitchen, slippers on his feet, an apron over his dress pants and collared shirt. What he was stirring in the deep pot smelled good; he called me over. "Y'ever had cow heel?" he asked. "My aunts talk about cow heel, but no. It's not really heel, is it?" I asked. He lifted the lid: the thing that bubbled up looked, indeed, like a slice of hoof. I grimaced. "What about souse?" asked Austin. I made another face. "No. And no black pudding with blood in it, either," I said. "Tchh, man," said Austin. "What kind o' Guyanese your mother raising?" He served the cow heel soup to us kids in Guelph, along with healthy doses of gin and vermouth, with a few other dishes that he was testing out for the book. That meal remains, to this day, the only experience of cow heel I've ever had. It tasted amazing—spicy, robust, and joyful—infused with the spirit of its cook.

CHAPTER 15

"The Wordshop of the Kitchen": Impressions of Austin Clarke and Paule Marshall

Asha Varadharajan[1]

Happenstance

Austin Clarke's writings are belated and still fugitive presences on my bookshelves. I have read his Barbadian and "Amurcan" contemporaries, George Lamming and Paule Marshall, respectively, with more care and attention. All three share a simultaneously fractious and poignant relation to Barbados, the place Marshall's father described as "some poor-behind little village buried in a sea of canes," a place he deemed hidden from and forgotten by God. Marshall's parents migrated from Barbados, but she was born in Brooklyn, New York. She often composes her novels in Barbados and Grenada, and "returns" to Barbados in her short fiction, which features characters and settings from her "native" land. Her reputation, however, is that of an American author, with complex relations to both the African-American and Caribbean literary traditions. This chapter forges a serendipitous link between Marshall's *Triangular Road: A Memoir* (2009), her short story, "Da-Duh, in Memoriam" (1967), and Clarke's *Growing Up Stupid Under the Union Jack* (1980), in a bid to see what their unaccustomed juxtaposition might elicit. Both Clarke and Marshall write from their respective locations in Canada and the US, thus fashioning Barbados in the light of an unsentimental nostalgia.

Diasporic life and consciousness tend to be imagined as a series of leavings, as embarking upon the new and the unknown, or as thresholds between a receding past and an uncertain future rather than conceived of as vivid, if ambiguous, returns to one's origins. I chose *Growing Up Stupid* deliberately, because it recounts a life when Canada "was a blur on [his] consciousness" (31) rather than Clarke's customary habitat. Marshall's *Triangular Road*, as its title suggests, straddles Africa, America, and the Caribbean uneasily; however, it, too, narrates a voyage in rather than a voyage out, weaving in and out of history and memory, as Clarke does.

My inspiration for teasing out unsuspected affinities between Clarke and Marshall was the latter's essay "From the Poets in the Kitchen." In it, she pays tribute to women as "unknown bards" in whose everyday speech she discovered beauty, poetry, and wisdom (5). This world, in which women were ubiquitous and men largely absent or distant, parallels that of Clarke's boyhood: men are cruel, inadequate, feckless, exploited, isolated, or dead. Clarke associates adult men with "the smear of illegitimacy" (121), the fear of abandonment and penury, the weakness for rum, and the brutal or preening exercise of authority, but women command love and awe. My curiosity was piqued by this strange bond between a male (often perceived as misogynist) writer, and a female one who self-consciously dropped the feminine ending from the original rendering of her name—substituting "Paule" for "Paulette"—in order to announce herself as the heir to a male poet, Paul Dunbar. How did they come to have so much in common? And what should I make of the significant differences in their retelling of "Bajan" body and spirit, geography and history, skin and identity? As Clarke muses in *Growing Up Stupid*, everybody has style, and the eloquence with which Marshall and Clarke exploit and transfigure the quotidian gives it both power and dignity.

Some days ago, I came upon a hardbound copy of Clarke's *More* in a second-hand bookshop for the princely sum of one dollar. I rushed in gleefully waving my five-dollar bill but the shopkeeper didn't have change and couldn't be bothered to get it, so she handed the book back to me, carelessly indicating I could have it for free. Her gesture and my initial pleasure at picking up a bargain gave me pause—surely the book should have been worth, well, more? I hope this essay is in some small fashion the more that Clarke's and Marshall's protagonists seek but don't always find.

"Bright as shite" (Clarke)

Paule Marshall remarks on her mother and her friends' penchant for "the antonym, the contradiction, the linking of opposites" so that "they gave one as much weight and importance as the other" ("From the Poets" 8). Marshall's sense that such a fragile reconciliation of opposites reflected these women's "very conception of reality" encapsulates the world of *Growing Up Stupid* too. Clarke, however (as Marshall knows writers do) sketches his world all the while "stretching, shading, deepening" the meaning of the compound of beautiful and ugly it connotes (9).

One has only to recall Clarke's searing description of the flogging he and his classmates receive from their headmaster "with the pre-soaked, pee-soaked fan belt from his wife's sewing machine" (9), accompanied by the "profundo of his voice" (145) raised in harmony with the rest of the school "like a choir of a cathedral" (7), to recognize both the unsettling character of this dualism and its beauty. The exhaustion of the boys is counterpointed by the headmaster's perspiring black skin "jewelled with beads" (9) as his violence finally comes to an end. If the book was simply peppered with such scenes of discipline and punishment, it might have become tedious. Clarke interrupts this tedium with the puckish attempts of the boys to replace the vicious bamboo rods with tamarind ones to soften the blow and with their dreams of vengeance with "bull-pistle" whips of their own while they wash feces from their legs and pants after yet another flogging. Moreover, Clarke punctuates the grandeur of this ritual violence with the inexplicable and frequent deaths of Barbadian men and boys. Some are lost at sea during the war; one boy trampled by a horse during the races is promptly forgotten when the next race begins; and the boy who boasts he can swim "like a shark and a half" is "drowned the first week of the next vacation" (32). Clarke renders the arbitrary and unjust fates of these men and boys as routine as the predictable violence of colonial education. He thus peoples the "streets which kicked up the dust of these men's former cocky independence" (12) while establishing the framework within which what his and Marshall's mothers call "cutting and contriving" (201)—surviving—acquires meaning.

"Furious with the father I continued helplessly to love" (Marshall)

Clarke asserts that the women never speak of the men until after they are dead, and even then, only fitfully. His own father appears merely as the man who stained the white of his mother's wedding dress and consigned him to the fate of a "bastard," and his stepfather, despite being an industrious man and the one who enables Clarke's mother to realize her dream of living in her own home, remains a shadowy figure in Clarke's narrative. Hidden among the pages of Clarke's memoir are glimpses of passionate and self-indulgent and even indolent Barbadian men, an indolence and recklessness born of "the pain and regret at becoming a man too soon" (118). The prospect of hard labour in the canefields and quarries, of functioning as the "bread-winner . . . when there was little bread" (118), or of eking out a living as a poorly paid and unsuitably clad civil servant goes a long way toward explaining Sam Burke, Paule Marshall's fascinating and elusive father.

Burke is a stowaway and illegal alien who abandons life under the harsh glare of the sun in the canefields of Barbados and Cuba because both have been transformed, as Marshall writes, into "a sugar bowl to sweeten England's tea" (*Road* 72). He arrives in Brooklyn and sweeps Marshall's mother, Adriana, off her feet. Burke never quite makes his peace with the "ignominy" of dreary labour while "the holy grail of his true calling continu[es] to elude him" (79). Burke's natty attire, his haughty refusal to stoop to what the world is willing to offer, his irrepressible charm and "antic" disposition, the hymns he bursts into to drown out his wife's scolding, his pleasure in women's bodies, and the tenderness with which he cooks his young daughter a soft-boiled egg, the taste of which remains unforgettable, make him a man who turns life into art, living it with all the flair and bravado he can muster (81). Marshall's description of herself in Adriana's accusatory tones as "*Hard-ears!*," "*Willful!*," and "*Own-ways!*" establishes her as her father's daughter, deaf to her mother's "Xanthippe"-like shrillness (83).

I surmise that Marshall's yearning for the father she loved but could not forgive prompts her to open *Triangular Road* with her abiding affection and respect for Langston Hughes, also a dapper dreamer with a taste for the good life and a habit of surprising her with thoughtful postcards and whimsical gifts. The difference, of course, is that this mentor-father amounted to something, fulfilling his dream rather than being condemned, like Burke, to defer it. At least in *Growing Up Stupid*, Clarke makes no mention of any such benevolent father figures (as opposed to brutalizing ones), except for his Latin master, Sleepy Smith, who taught them "who they were" and encouraged them to dream "dreams of reality" and to wear their pips "with pride and dignity" (198). This mention of Smith is so fleeting, however, that it sticks out in Clarke's memoir, which is otherwise steeped in the "honeyed" voices and "soft, satin" bodies of women.

"Soully-gals" (Marshall)

The fusion of "soul: spirit" with the "body, flesh, the visible self" animates the disturbing, irreverent, and sensuous scenes in

Clarke's memoir that feature the labouring, nurturing, and desirable bodies of women ("From the Poets" 9). Marshall certainly focuses on women selling their domestic labour to white households for a pittance before coming home to cook and clean for their families in turn. However, her emphasis on the economic continuities of life in the Islands and in Brooklyn, where their race, sex, poverty, and foreignness render Bajans even more invisible than their African-American counterparts, lacks the texture of Clarke's depictions of female lives irradiated by labour as it does the pleasure, spectacle, and transport the bounty of female bodies offers. In contrast, Marshall's young womanhood is dogged by Adriana's fears of her becoming a "little wring-tail" (concubine) revealing the luxury afforded Clarke of observing everything from budding to Oedipal female sexuality (*Road* 94).

I understand why Clarke's representation of female sexuality and religiosity and the violence implicit in both may be perceived as stereotypical or sexist, but I think such a view misses his appreciation for what Marshall would describe as "scandalous" and "independent" women who "[take their] pleasure at will" ("From the Poets" 8). The scene in which Sister Thomas seduces the young Clarke—it remains ambiguous whether this is simply an ecstatic moment of spiritual possession—induces unease, no doubt, because her predatory desire is fulfilled with such artlessness, but is also a comic rendering of the laying on of hands that makes healing synonymous with orgasm. The "catfight" that no doubt draws the ire of sensitive readers is also leavened by its function as a ritual catharsis of sorts, exposing secrets that bind a community even closer together in their new-found knowledge, while reducing men and boys capable of looking at women to being unworthy of touching them. Because Clarke also depicts the constraints upon female existence such as illiteracy, bent backs, and ragged knees, these luscious, expressive, and uncontainable bodies could be seen as the equivalent of the "spoken word" that Marshall insists is the "only weapon at [the] command" of the women she knows ("From the Poets" 7).

"Encountering a past that is not past"
(Christina Sharpe)

Clarke and Marshall (en)gender a surprising reversal of expectations. Clarke appeals to the senses while Marshall, at least in this work, is more cerebral than visceral, writing with restraint and subtlety rather than exuberance. This may be the consequence of the delicate negotiation of proximity and distance in both works. Marshall describes how the women remember Barbados as "Poor—poor but sweet " ("From the Poets" 6). The makeshift existence of the poor in Barbados parallels the slipperiness of self-worth in America and, as Marshall explains, the talk of women "[restores] them to a sense of themselves" (6). Their memories of Barbados, however, are not hers, which is why her journey requires her to reconstruct a public past to which she can lay claim rather than encounter a private ancestry to which she can pledge fealty.

Growing Up Stupid dwells on details that make memory and experience coalesce: the sweat that takes "its wet awful-smelling toll" (133) on Sister Christopher's body; the "greasy and delicious" (65) food his mother cooks; the coachmen dressed up like "fat cockroaches" (194); the squirming, wriggly centipedes that terrorize them; the saving of always too-tight shoes for special occasions; the year it takes to pay off four rolls of cloth; the interminable and painstaking copying of Latin texts and translations. The inglorious everyday is the source of Barbados's sweetness, and yet those details don't add up to a picture of abjection and deprivation—one leaves Clarke's memoir brimming with choice morsels of phrases, rather than a world emptied of meaning and hope.

In Marshall's search for her origins, for a kinship denied her by the father who disowns his past, she claims as her "progenitors" "the incorrigibles in Barbados" "who had somehow withstood the whipping post and the pillory," as well as the "negroes" "led off to centuries of John Henry work," Olaudah Equiano, and the drowned victims of the Zong massacre (*Road* 111). Her writing acquires the sensory quality of Clarke's in describing the condition of the chattel cargo that landed in Richmond, Virginia—the "stench, the running sores, the caked shit"—letting her imagination do the work of observation (48). Marshall assumes the burden of a history she did not experience, abstracts from a past she discovers but does not know, and situates herself in the afterlives of slavery. These afterlives are manifested both in the irony and insouciance of her Jewish editor eagerly anticipating her visit to the slave plantation and in her invention of a historical and aesthetic legacy of militants and poets to which she can belong comfortably. For Clarke, on the contrary, growing up Barbadian but educated in English history and manners requires him to make that history "a part of [him]." The "beauty and shame and sensuality" (167) of life in Barbados become "the history and civilization of [his] village" (168). In other words, Clarke memorializes the past while Marshall re-visions it.

This is nostalgia with a sting in its tail, however. Marshall's task is that of excavating and re-membering a history buried in dusty tomes that nobody ever reads in her university library, absent from the education she received in schools, ignored by libraries where she is embarrassed to ask for "Negro" writers, and denied by those who live in Virginia. That Marshall first delivered the material in *Triangular Road* as a series of lectures in 2005 tells its own tale of America's successes in coming to terms with its past.

Two moments in *Growing Up Stupid* are lodged in my memory. First, the narrator-Clarke witnesses a white boy kissing a black dog, a sight which makes him throw up. The narrator informs us that the boys believed dogs were taught by white owners to eat Black boys alive. This explains the fear fuelling his nausea but the nausea is also fuelled by his unconscious identification with the black dog fawning on its white owner, for which it is rewarded with a kiss. Second, we learn that the posh neighbourhood in Barbados, Belleville, shines white and bright because of Black hands that scrub and polish, change diapers and slap white bottoms, and induce white orgasms "through love or through rape" (194). Clarke's description of Belleville as "the place against which we measured our misery, and our mobility" (194) expands the implications of the shocking equivalence he establishes between rape and love in a colonial environment. The cruel Black headmaster who always wears white, Marshall's character Mr. Watson who spends his life savings earned in America to build a "replica of a white planter's great house" in Barbados (a "colonial showpiece" in which he would have been forbidden to step foot in his youth), and the "lucky clear-skinned few" who could ride through canefields in which a field woman could "give up her body in order to keep her job and feed her children," are painful reminders of how history and tyranny repeat themselves and "the slime of poverty" leaves "the people living in the castles of their skins." Such deprivation fosters imitation of one's betters, thus ruining one's chances of both freedom from want and freedom from slavery.

But if Belleville was an inescapable "reference point" for Barbadians' misery, its magnificence is also theirs "to conquer" (197). A fine sentiment on Clarke's part, perhaps, but Marshall remains uncertain at the end of her voyage that guilt, shame, and sorrow can be transcended or that her visit to parts of the Caribbean and Africa truly constitutes a gesture of reclamation, reconciliation, and forgiveness that redeems her American present. Clarke's mood is more hopeful in that the past sustains rather than torments him as he embarks upon the new phase of his life in Canada.

"An insistence on existing" (Sharpe)

I want to end on a speculative note. Both Clarke and Marshall have the gift of transforming physical death into figurative life, of resuscitating social death in the loving arms of remembrance, and of turning memoir into a reflection of and on history. But their fictions also contain compelling meditations on what eludes the imagination and recedes from memory, what haunts and mocks their efforts, what continues to blind them, and what is stubbornly absent once love loses its fervour and releases its hold. In an enigmatic disquisition on perspective in *Growing Up Stupid*, the narrator-Clarke comments wryly that "the chattel house is merely a section of the plantation house" (150). Clarke's bleak humour casts doubt on not only the clarity of the past but even its visibility, just as Marshall abandons historical facts for the modest truths of fiction at the end of *Triangular Road*. The emphasis on repetition rather than transcendence, and upon obscurity rather than illumination, recalls the ambiguity of Toni Morrison's rueful conclusion in *Beloved* that "[slavery] was not a story to pass on" (315).

Marshall's "To Da-Duh, in Memoriam" is the counterpart to Clarke's radical uncertainty. In it, she traces her grandmother's contours, her face "stark and fleshless as a death-mask" and her countenance "distorted by an ancient abstract sorrow" (96). Marshall's characterization transforms her grandmother into darkness visible, and all her appearances occur in the play of sunlight and darkness, one blinding and the other impenetrable. While it is tempting to imagine Da-Duh as an indomitable presence, this is the story of her inevitable defeat by a self-immolating colonial past and of her trampling by the "thunderous tread" of machines and skyscrapers in the diasporic present. The narrator lives not in the wake of her life but in the shadow of her death, unable to restore the vibrancy of the tropical landscape in art or revive it in memory. The story's title connotes a letter to an absent and silent addressee followed immediately by the words "in Memoriam," already mourning the figure whom affection cannot embrace or resurrect. Even Clarke's resort to tangible details such as wet lips and a toothless smile to fix his grandmother in loving memory appears as an afterthought in a portrait composed largely in the subjunctive mood. Marshall's world is infinitely diminished by the memory of Da-Duh while Clarke's "poor and foolish" grandmother is elevated in the world's eyes by the Latinate love he expresses: "*Miriam amo*" (191).

These works raise the question of whether and how fiction can or might remember, atone for, abide with what Christina Sharpe calls *subjected lives*, invite vulnerability but resist abjection, and invoke love.

Note

1 I'd like to thank Michael Bucknor and Lisa Brown for suggesting that I compare *Growing Up Stupid* and *Triangular Road*.

CHAPTER 16

Of Kin and Kind

Marquita Smith

In his article "'Our words spoken among us, in fragments': Austin Clarke's Aesthetics of Crossing," Paul Barrett recalls a bold statement from a 1996 interview with Dionne Brand and Rinaldo Walcott in which Clarke proclaimed, "there are no Canadian critics qualified to look at the things I write, in the sense of having a sensitive feeling towards what I write" (90). When I was first approached about contributing to a collection in honour of the late Austin Clarke, I thought, *I am an outsider. An interloper.* I had to remind myself of the diasporic view of Blackness that was so important to his work and his insistence on making space for Blackness where it was tacitly told it should not be. As I thought about what this "sensitive feeling" might be for me as a Black American, I returned again and again to feeling a kind of kinship.

My introduction to Clarke came in a graduate course at McMaster University focusing on "the interpretive frameworks we bring to our interpretations of Canadian texts" and, more broadly, the politics of literary canonization. In a particularly rancorous seminar session on *The Meeting Point*, we came to a discussion of the scene in which the head nurse, a Black woman named Priscilla, works to distinguish herself in the eyes of her white colleagues from another Black woman, Estelle, who is suffering a miscarriage. Though she was part of the welcoming party for Estelle's arrival in Canada, Priscilla comes to model that unique blend of anti-Blackness and sexism that cuts deeply at Black women. ("Another black whore! . . . They don't even have any shame!" [248] she declares.) At this point, a white woman in the room pondered if this was, in fact, true. Were there not "two kinds of black women" (248), as Priscilla suggested? In this moment, the seemingly innocent tone in this woman's voice made clear the power of Clarke's work to lay anti-Blackness in Canada bare. The paradox of such a literary rendering of the insidious nature of racism was lost in the woman's interpretation. In that graduate seminar, I quickly learned how anti-Blackness can continue to be reproduced with minuscule difference.

Today, more than a hundred and fifty years into "Canada," many are eager to celebrate the benevolence of the nation, especially in comparison to the United States and the current Trump regime. However, such comparisons too easily cast shadows that can obscure discomforting truths. Certainly, my own engagement with Clarke's work sprung from my interest in exploring transnational Blackness. I once described Clarke's Toronto Trilogy (*The Meeting Point, Storm of Fortune,* and *The Bigger Light*) as an exploration of the limitations of deploying American-centric models of Blackness and political resistance. At the time, my reading of the trilogy focused on what I saw as a growing disillusionment with such models of racial alliance for its characters. But this was only the beginning of my growing understanding of one of the most important themes present in Clarke's work. His work does not enable a comparison to the political climate of the United States that paints Canada as an accepting multicultural nation, and thus elides its own history of white supremacy.

Reading Clarke thoughtfully means confronting the problem of anti-Blackness in Canada as a specific, local one that, though sharing elements of American-style racism, manifests itself in other insidious ways. Clarke's body of work has consistently excavated the cost of white supremacy for Black lives. I am reminded of it each time I return to Toronto. I recall that the only time I have (yet) been called "nigger" to my face occurred on a packed

TTC train. I remember this cost each time I revisit the sensation of being in that packed train car full of white, deathly silent faces that communicated so much with so little. I think back to that room full of future educators and public servants, many of whom would carry forth ideas of Canadian righteousness, unmarred by the literary representation of Black Canadians' quotidian experiences of anti-Black racism and discrimination. I ruminate on the difference between acts of kindness that can serve as important interventions and the inaction of passive consent.

Clarke's oeuvre urges us to recognize and reckon with the histories of colonization and enslavement that link *here* to *there*, *past* to *present*. His work requires seeing these entanglements not as signs of Canada's exemplary fairness or its status as an open society, but as a progeny of the same notions of race that continuously give life to white supremacy elsewhere. Anti-Black racism in Canada may not seem as intensely spectacular as the American variety, but it is nonetheless an extension of the shared legacy of colonization that binds Canada, Britain, and the United States. In *The Meeting Point*, Clarke urges us to confront this ugly inheritance, to resist the impulse to simplistically trade one kind of space for another. It is not enough to bestow awards and honours upon the talented and well-deserving. True tribute to Clarke's work requires facing the reality of racism in Canada, which is uncomfortable, inculpatory, and challenging.

CHAPTER 17

The Robber

Austin Clarke

This unpublished story offers a dark comedic take on depictions of Black men in Canada, feelings of Black invisibility, and the anxieties of Black male sexuality. Here, the social invisibility that many of Clarke's characters experience is (perhaps) rendered literal and Clarke's engagement with Ellison's Invisible Man *is evident. This actual feeling of invisibility gives the protagonist an idea about how to be seen in a society that cannot recognize him. The story is at once light-humoured yet suffused with the dark undercurrent of the feeling of suffering and marginalization of Black life in Canada. The first-person narrative voice speaking in nation language is typical of Clarke's short fiction in the 1970s and '80s.*

Loftus stand-up at the same street corner Monday to Friday, from nine in the morning till three in the afternoon, studying a bank. The bank was across the street. Loftus stand-up so long in one place that he start to feel he was a telephone post growing outta the ground. And seeing that it was in winter that Loftus first start this standing-up in the street, watching the bank, his feet start feeling like two pieces of icicles that was sprouting-out outta the corner of Sin George and Bloor Street.

He did not want to call the cold effect of his standing-up there by another name, to suggest how frozen-up his body was. But he couldn't remember if the right word was "staligmites," which he thought was cold things hanging-down, or something else. It was a very big thing with him about the correct name for his standing-up in that posture, cause seeing that he was a very particular kind o' man, he promise himself many times whilst standing-up there, that he going walk cross by the big Newniversity Library that they had just build on the same Sin George Street, to check-out, if really in truth, "staligmites" was the correct word, if that was the word that stand-for ice growing-down or for ice growing-up outta the ground.

Whilst he was watching the bank, all kinds o' people pass and watch Loftus standing-up there. And not one body amongst all them multitudes o' people didn't even had the presence of mind to tell Loftus that he couldn't or shouldn't stand-up there, as the case may be. Out of all them people that pass, none of them *see* Loftus: and Loftus, when he think of the situation, decide that he must be invisible.

Only one man stop and ask Loftus, after the second day, if he didn't live nowhere, if he didn't know he was loitering or dis-turbing the peace, or being a cumbrance to the procedure of pedestrians. And that one man who say so, was a police. A black police from the West Indies. This police had drive-up and stop beside o' Loftus in the motto-car, and had hold his head outta the car and say, "Hey you! You blocking the procedure of the pedes-trians! You blocking the pedestrians from passing. Move along, and don't let me see you . . ."

Loftus went to move along. But when he do so, and try to lift his right foot, whiching is how he always move-off from one loca-tion that he want to move-off from, to the next location, be-Christ, the foot won't move at all. Loftus had turn into a "staligmite." Loftus foot stick-on 'pon the ice. And the more Loftus try, the more the foot like it turn-into a piece of "staligmite," in truth.

That was when Loftus did first start thinking he should know the exact phraseology to connote everything he do in regards to this standing-up procedure watching the bank. A lotta motto-cars was in the same lane as the motto-car with the black police in it; and they start blowing and honking their horns and saying that the police is the first ones to break the law, and so on; so the police get vex as hell with the pedestrians in the motto-cars blowing their horns in his ears, and he step on the excelerator and speed-off. But if there wasn't such a commotion on behalf of the public, the police would have put his hand in Loftus arse, for hampering the procedure of the pedestrians, there and then. As a matter of fact, just as the police screel-off in the cruiser, Loftus think he hear him say, "I coming-back for your arse!" But Loftus wasn't frighten for no police, though.

Loftus uses to be a man who spend a lotta time in the Reference Library 'pon College Street. And he get to know all the rights that he have in this strange land and that he living in now, and he know too, all the wrongs that the public and the police in this cold place could perform against him. Years ago, Loftus was just another fella from the West Indies who did come up here to go through for Law. But a girl from Guyana trick Loftus. She trick Loftus by having a next man. And bram! the unfaithfulness went to Loftus head and cause Loftus to start walking-'bout the place as of he was going-off-in-the-head, like a insane mad-man. Fellas who went to the Newniversity along with Loftus years ago, still walking-'bout and talking 'bout how Norma the Guynese girl trick Loftus. And when they see Loftus now, walking-'bout like a mad-man, in this dreamy-dreamy state, they would walk fast and pass-out Loftus; or else they would rush-cross the next side of the street and don't notice Loftus at all, at all. Loftus was invisible to them, too. But if they was to have *see* Loftus first, bram! fast-fast so they stop, and make a turn-around right in the road and gone! But Loftus didn't care.

Loftus didn't give one shite if none o' them ever speak to him again. Because he had one thing in mind: ". . . cause, gorblummuh! I going make them *see* me! I going do something to *make* them see me!" In the rest o' life, previous and in the past, Loftus was a compound failure.

And this is how, if during them days after the fellas stop seeing Loftus, and after the Guynese girl stop seeing Loftus through the trick Loftus find-out that she play on him, you was to walk-down Bloor Street by Sin George, you would see this tall black man standing-up on the sidewalk right in the procedure of pedestrians, watching a bank on the next corner.

Loftus become so popular as a landmark that a ewespaper-fella with a camera, stop one day and take a picture of Loftus, and put the picture the next morning, on the front page, under a headline that read, "The sights and scenes of the City." And during that same morning, when all the usual people and some people that never uses to pass there before all the time, pass, the people going-in and coming-out outta the bank, not one of them people didn't even as much as stand up and open their mouth, and say with a kind o'surprise, "Heyyyyyy! You is the fella what is the sights and scenes of this City!" Be-Christ, Loftus like he is really a invisible man, in truth, yuh! But Loftus didn't care. Loftus couldn't give a shite 'bout the picture nor the people who didn't see him nor read 'bout him in the ewespaper.

Really and truly, though, Loftus did getting a little tired standing-up watching bank, dress-off in his big brown long army winter coat, and in shoes that had-in three holes in one shoe, nothing on Loftus head, and not much inside Loftus stomach, cause things was rough-rough in them days. Loftus arse getting cold cold cold, too; cause he haven't got-on no underwears; and with the winter crawling-through Loftus body like how castor oil uses to crawl-through his bowels every first Sunday of the month when he was a little boy back in the West Indies, he really convince himself that he turning into a "staligmite."

But still, Loftus stand-up and standup-up; watch and watch, and take notes in his mind, concerning the operation of the bank. He had figure-out the whole plan by himself. The plan hit Loftus sudden one night when he was in bed and couldn't sleep, cause the cold was passing-through holes in the window and through the thinness of the blanket he had over him covering him from the coldness, like a cover. Everything was passing through Loftus in them days: the cold, the "staligmites," the eyes and the stares.

"Jesus Christ!," Loftus should out; and he stand-up straight as a icicle in bed.

He get so damn vex that he had waste so much time as a compound-interest failure: working-off his arse as a civil servant licking stamps, after he stop bursting his brains over the Law; driving taxi to gather material and meet womens cause he did want to be a writer once before too, and did fail at that; driving a messenger-van to see what the inside o' the characters house look like; every conceivable task and occupation Loftus meddle-in and fail in in them days, when he was looking for something to become. And every evening, drunk or sober, in them same days, Loftus uses to be the first man present in the Hall down by the UNIA Hall, where they have a picture of Marcus Garvey and one of Malcolm X, and a charcoal sketch o' Martin Luther King. In them days, Loftus was a big revolutionary. Every cock-fight and demonstration didn't well organize, before Loftus wasn't marching in it. Every petition that was ever draw-up in a petition, have Loftus signature on it. Loftus picket, sit-in, siddown, lie-down, hauled his arse all over the people road and the Queen's highway, private property and embassy, and once, it take four big real white-police to move Loftus from in front of the American Consulate. So being on the front page in the Sights-and-scenes-of-the-City column wasn't nothing new to Loftus. That didn't make Loftus into no celebrity. Cause the RCMP and 'Merican FBI and various other kinds o' undressed and plainclothes police did already take a million pictures o' Loftus during them Civil Rights days when all Loftus was a failure, cause Loftus wasn't doing nothing wrong saving standing-up for his rights. All that brand o' water with a evil taste in it, pass under the bridge as Loftus jump-up like a "staligmite" that night, in winter, when the plan hit him.

Plain business Loftus mean now. He intend to perform a act in this place *bound* to make people see him. Loftus even remember something outta one o' them books he had was to read in Latin back in the West Indies, and how there was this fella by the name o' Hannibal who was such a celebrity, and who uses to be invisible like Loftus, and who put on a act, and had all the people in the Germanic and Hispanic and Gallic tribes telling their thrildren for centuries afterwards 'bout Hannibal; Hannibal was such a celebrity that a nurse-maid uses to tell a child, "I am going to call Hannibal for your arse, if you don't stop playing the arse and eat this baby-food, hear?" And the thrildrens uses to scream for blue murder, and then keep quiet quiet as a lamb, like the lamb that Mary had, a little one that she uses to walk-'bout with in a fleet of wool. That was the brand o' man Hannibal was. Loftus say, "Man, that man Hannibal was a real gorilliphant!"

But what really did make Loftus really and truly want to launch this attack 'pon the bank, was that after living-through thirteen years o' protest and demonstration and failure and he didn't become no celebrity; and that since they only uses to print pictures o' black people getting beat-up by the police; or else living in a slums or a ghetto as they christen it on the television; and since he never see nothing so on the front page of a ewespaper; and having this phrase from *Caesar Gallic War* or from *Livy* flash through his mind that night when he stand-up like a piece o' iron make out of ice, "Hannibal in occulo altero Alpes transgressersomething . . ." is when he decide to rob a bank. And bram! He work out a plan.

"Pure discrimination," he tell a fella, in confidence, after the idea hit him three weeks ago.

"Discrimination? You now find-out 'bout that?"

"Discrimination," Loftus tell him again.

"And I suppose you know that the police is the worse . . ."

"Worse what?"

"Suppose a police was to catch you, one o' these days!"

"How?"

"With a computer."

"Have you ever hear of a black bank robber yet?"

"Well, now that you mention that, I could tell you that the odds is . . . but I can't *see* you pulling off a thing like that. I just can't *see* it, I just can't *see*, a West Indian . . ."

"Is discrimination is not having a black bank robber," Loftus say. He know that his plan waterproof. He has stand-up at that corner, rub his hand, one 'gainst the next, the cold turning him into a "staligmite" and then the same cold turn-round and thaw him out, going through all these changes o' permutations of precipitation and metamorphobias, and this blasted fella going tell him some damn foolishness 'bout a computer. "You want to know how I know that this plan is watertight?"

"Well, when the water hit it, I going watch you getting wet, or come and visit you in Don Jail, boy!" And the fella get offa the chair and stand-up to leave.

But before the fella left, Loftus shout-out while he was leaving, "Invisibility, old man! Invisibility!"

"Indivisi-*what*?"

"Bility!"

And that was the plan. Loftus realize through experience stretching thirteen years that he had the ability to be invisible. Cause look: psychology and sociology and race relations tell Loftus something about himself, from the other point o' view; that base on certain experiences, he *must* be rass-hole invisible, cause nobody don't *see* him! When that psychological truth hit him, Loftus went wild in the Reference Library searching for a particular book to back-up the psychology concerning the ins and outs in regards to this invisible-thing.

"I looking for a certain book," he say to the librarian.

"What about one by Fanon? *Black Skin, White Masks?*"

"I read that."

"Would *Prospero and Caliban* . . . ?"

"Fuck that!" The way Loftus pronounce the words, the grey-hair lady didn't understand too good, cause him being a West Indian who naturally can't speak the King's English like a librarian; so she merely smile and went on looking for a book for Loftus.

"There's some very nice books on the Negro in America."

Loftus isn't no Negro in America; Loftus is a plain ordinary man who come in a library to find a particular book, so he don't know what the shite this intelligent grey-hair librarian-lady talking 'bout a Negro in America. But he didn't say nothing this time, so she went on looking, stopping to touch a book, and look-back to see how Loftus react, and all the time, Loftus following the lady hand and looking over her shoulders, when all of a sudden, Loftus see the book he was looking for, all the time. Loftus snatch the book from offa the shelf, and he hold the book soft in his hand, and read the title over and over. He sign out the book, and gone straight home.

He close all the curtains, lock the door to his room, take the phone offa the hook, and start reading. *The Psychology Of The Absurd!* Loftus start reading this book like how he uses to try to read the Law; and when he put it down, he did reach the end. When you see Loftus standing-up by Bloor and Sin George, betwixt the hours of nine and three on a Monday, Tuesday, Wednesday and Thursday; and from nine to six on a Friday, well it mean that Loftus already went through *The Psychology Of The Absurd* once already for that particular day. And when he gone back home, after a hard day's work standing-up looking at the bank, it isn't to cook nor eat nor to go listening to jazz nor to go out and old-talk with the fellas; gorblummuh, is reading Loftus gone home to do. When he was studying Law, is that kind o' pressure-reading Loftus uses to do. Loftus eyes did turn red red as a cherry since from them days with the Law books. But them days was empty days. Them was days with torts and habeas corpus and failure; wills and testaments and conveniences and headaches. Now, is pure dollars and sense Loftus reading 'bout.

In all, Loftus did spend three weeks looking at the bank. And he spend four weeks studying *The Psychology Of The Absurd.*

"*Hannibal in altero occulo Alpes transfresserimus est*" come back in his mind walking down Bloor one day with a lotta people in the sidewalk, and this big man walk right up to Loftus and he was carrying a big parcel and he walk right over Loftus and nearly trample Loftus and the man pick up the parcel and say, "Sorry, sir. I didn't see you."

And Loftus study all the ins and outs of how people would walk when they come out from outta the bank and their bank account is overdrawn or if it look so; how some people don't smile when they go into a bank to put money on a bank; how some people does look round quick quick to the left and to the right when they drawing-off a lotta money offa the bank; how one o' the mans from Brinks does get nervous and hold-on 'pon the gun tight tight tight and look to the right and then to the left and pat the money bag like if it is the bottom of a woman he have his eyes on, when he drive-up in the van; and how the next fella does run-in the bank ahead o' him with two guns holding like guns: everything, every particular thing concerning a bank and the goings-on in this particular bank, Loftus memorize. Loftus ready now.

The night before, A Thursday, Loftus put-back the phone back on the hook, and he call-up the same fella who didn't understand the terminology "invisibility." The fella visit Loftus as Loftus ask him, eager to laugh at Loftus and of course to fire a couple o' liquors in the meantime, cause all the time, in spire of all this studyation, Loftus didn't forget to fire a regular liquor—three or four scotches that he uses to drink every night, by himself, to put some spirits and heat in the thorax, as he uses to call his body.

"How the plan, man?" the fella say, not really wanting to hear no damn plan 'bout robbing no blasted bank. His mind on the level of the bottle.

"The *mind*, man!" Loftus tell him. If the mind right, gor-blummuh, the body *must* tick over like a machine! Mind over matter, man."

The fella start to laugh. "Now, if I was going to rob a bank, I would make sure that I have a alibi. Like in the movies. When I get the alibi work-out, then I would plan the robbery. The next thing is to get a getaway car. I would leave the getaway car running. Just round the corner. I go in the bank. Stick up the bank. Rush out. Get in the getaway. And I get-away!"

"In prison?"

"Or. Lissen to this next plan, then. You go in the bank. In broad daylight. You go in. With a mask on your face. With a black mask. Like in the movies. Nobody can't recognize who you is with a black mask on your face. Then, outside, you have *two* getaway cars. One is a big lorry or a truck. You park this big long-distance truck round the corner. The doors in the back you leave open. Then you have the next getaway car, the second getaway car, running. That one park behind the truck. You have a piece o' board, a big piece o' wood or a plan. Or something. And you place that in a certain position so that the jeep could drive up in the truck. When you drive the jeep right in the truck, you lock the truck doors, change-out outta your bank robbing clothes, and walk through the door of the truck, and stand-up and watch the police looking for the bank robber . . ."

Loftus didn't know what to say, so he start laughing. "What time would you rob a bank if you was going to rob a bank?"

"Five on a Friday."

"When there is a No-Parking signs on the street? You is a ass or you is a ass?"

"Six then."

"Banks close at six on Fridays."

"Oh!"

The fella couldn't think about no good way to rob a bank, so he start talking 'bout unemployment instead.

After a while, Loftus say he was tired, so he ask the fella to leave. When the fella leave, Loftus went-in a drawer, and take-out a small parcel and put it in one of the two inside pockets of the big long brown army coat. He take off his clothes and get in the bed, naked because he did want to suffer the inconvenience the whole night before, so he won't be careless the next morning. He wasn't even nervous 'bout doing the ting. And he had a dream, although he didn't sleep too good: *he is Hannibal crossing the Alps with twenty thousand solders and after he cross the Alps he cross a river and when eh come out on the other side of the bank and he has every man of those twenty thousand.* Loftus think and think 'bout this dream, and the more he think, the more difficult the dream was to understand, cause Loftus was never a soldier; he never even was a Boy Scout, so he couldn't understand all this damn foolishness 'bout rivers and Alps and soldiers and other logistics.

"Could it mean twenty thousand years?" But begin as how he was a ex-Law student, he realize that no judge couldn't give a first-offender twenty thousand years. Days maybe. But that couldn't be the interpretation o' the dream, at all.

But he was still worrying 'bout this dream even when he was standing-up next morning, Friday, around ten o'clock on the corner of Sin George and Bloor watching the bank cross the road, and still the meaning didn't come. The morning was so damn cold that he get frighten that his feet would really turn into "staligmites" in truth. And since he had to walk cross the road before he could go inside the bank to rob it, he start walking up and down to keep the cold circulating through his feet so that he won't turn-into a black piece o' ice. And he start laughing loud when he think 'bout that: imagine what he would look like, as a big tall piece o' black ice!

"Wonder if I would still be invisible, as ice!" he ask himself. But when he went to answer-back himself, the only thing that come outta his mouth, was something that look like smoke. It did really getting cold.

The time come. Loftus pound both feets on the cold pavement. A shiver went right through his body like a shot o' Jamaica white rum. He repeat in his mind, as he cross-over the street, the parts of *The Psychology Of The Absurd* that he had pick-out for this test o' invisibility. He remember the technique. And he laugh. And he take the thing outta the parcel outta his pocket and put it on.

Inside the bank, there was ten people, mens and womens in three lines. Loftus look for the prettiest white woman behind the counter, and when he decide that the black-hair one with the large blue eyes was the most prettiest and the most youngest, because all three was really young and pretty women and young ladies with blue eyes, he went in that line.

When he get second from the girl, there was five people left in the bank. Four womens was sitting down at desses behind the counter. A big door that look like the door to a big safe was open. But he couldn't see no money in the safe, though . . . The manager was in a office that had MANAGER write-down on the glass; and the door was shut and he couldn't see through the door cause the glass was like if snow was painted all over it. But he could see the manager as a shadow whenever the body in the office move.

He right on top of the woman now.

"Good morning, sir!" she said, as if she was singing a song for Loftus. "May I help you this morning, please?"

First time in his thirteen years that any bank-woman ever address him so. Is a nice way to address a person by, he conclude. So he know that he was correct, psychologically-speaking, to wear the thing that was in the parcel, which as he had plan, he put on just before he enter the bank door.

"Cold enough this morning for you, sir?" Birds coming-outta the woman mouth.

"It's cool!"

"And what can we do for you this morning?"

"Can you see me?" Loftus ask her, and he move-back from the teller-woman and the counter.

The woman hold-up slightly outta the chair and lean-over a bit, and when she look, she say "Nooo!" in a voice soft as a dove would say it, and as if she was going to faint. She speak in such a soft voice that nobody to the left or nobody to the right didn't hear what she say, neither in front the counter, or behind the counter with her.

"Gimme all!" Loftus say, trying to talk like a bank robber, or like a gorilliphant, in a gruff voice. But the tone come-out real soft. "Give it to me! All!"

The girl now, like she really going to faint. And trying not to look at what Loftus show she and ask she to look at, but wanting to look at it all the same, and in-between all this confusion in her mind, not wanting to let nobody else in the bank, either in front the counter or behind the counter with her, share in this sight, she put her hand right inside the place where the root of all evil is, deep down inside her drawers, and bring-up all the money she had inside there.

"Thanks," Loftus say, and just as he was going to turn and walk-out outta the bank, the nice pretty woman-teller fall-down over the counter, and the other tellers say, "Ohhhh!," and the people in the lines say, "Oh my gosh!"

Loftus continue walking-way from the counter, and when he turn his back to everybody, he take-off the thing that he had put-on his face. He put it in his pocket, and join-back in the same line. But before he join-back in the line, he make sure that he button-back-up his trousers.

It only a take a little time to revive the teller back to life. And when she was revive-back, and seeing real, like before, Loftus was standing-up in front o' she.

Loftus remain standing-up for about three or four or five seconds before she even look up at him. She start getting busy counting money and doing things with bills and elastic bands, and when she did finish doing these things with the elastic bands, she say without really looking-up at Loftus eyes, but looking at Loftus as if she was looking *through* Loftus, "What?" She say "What?" in the same voice that a woman in the personnel office down at *Maclean's Magazine* did use to Loftus when Loftus went for a job, which as he expect, he didn't get.

"What?"

"Change."

She take up the twenty dollar bill, and without asking Loftus how he want this change he talking 'bout, she break-up the twenty dollar bill, without looking in Loftus face, and she push three fives and five ones in front o' Loftus.

Loftus turn and walk-back outside. The sun did come out by now. And it was bright bright like in the West Indies back home. It was like life was growing outta the snow. He walk-cross the street and stand-up at the same corner of Sin George and Bloor, as if nothing didn't happen, whiching it didn't, because he was invisible. And he stand-up there with the money inside his pocket, and watch the people go-in and come-out outta the bank, and from ten-thirty till six-something when the bank close, Loftus didn't even worry to count how much money he get from the teller-woman.

He stand up there *just* to see what going happen. "*In altero occulo*" pass through his mind. And he put his hand inside his pocket and pull-out a mask of a white-man face with one eye missing. He throw it in a white-thing that was mark KEEP THE CITY CLEAN. IT IS YOUR CITY AND MINE. Loftus didn't even know before-now, that the city did belongs to him, too.

Just after seven o'clock a motto-car with the West Indian police in it, screel to a stop in front of the bank. And right after that, a ambulance with DEPARTMENT OF MENTAL HEALTH write-down on it, and in white, pull-up behind the police motto-car. Two men with white coats get-out with a roll-up stretcher in their hand. A man come to the bank door and open for the three of them. Loftus was standing-up like he always uses to stand-up on the corner. Then they bring-out a person on the stretcher, a woman she looked like, judging from the length of the hair. And before the ambulance drive-off, two more motto-cars with police, went in the bank. Loftus remain standing-up till everybody come-out outta the bank, including the bank-people and the police.

Loftus must have remain standing-up till everybody come-out outta the bank and went home, including the bank-people, the police and the public. And then he went home. He take-off the army coat, and hang it up. And then he pour himself a scotch.

"I gotta take-back this book to the Library in the morning," he say to himself, as he take-off all his clothes and get in the bed. It did get really cold that night, and he didn't want to sleep too well cause he did want to think 'bout how easy it was to be invisible. And between sleeping and waking and turning-over on his side, a dream come to him: *a young beautiful woman with blue eyes and black hair was sitting-down on a bench and he was standing-up in*

*front of her and somebody call-out his name, "Loftus, your turn, boy!"
and he move-forward and when he move-forward the woman who was
sitting down in front of him to get-up and walk straight down in front of
him get-up and walk straight to him as if she was going to walk through
him, and before he had time to shuffle outta the woman way, he look back
and find out that she had pass right through him as if he didn't exist as
a substance at all.*

"Jesus Christ!"

It was the fella who uses to come to drink-out Loftus liquor,
addressing Loftus. Loftus never lock his door, so the fella had
come right in and was standing-up over Loftus. Loftus was really
mad cause the fella interrupt the dream, and Loftus did want to
know how this dream was going to turn-out.

"Twenty-fucking-thousand-dollar bills!"

The fella drop a usedpaper on top o' Loftus. "The *same* bank
I tell you I couldn't see you robbing. I couldn't see you doing a
thing like this. The man that rob that bank is a fucking genius!
Lissen to what they say 'bout that bank robber: . . . *blah-blah-
blah . . . a young female bank teller who has been working at the Bloor-St.
George branch of the Bank of Commerce for four years, yesterday went
berserk and then lost her power of speech before she could identify a man
who demanded twenty thousand dollars from her till. Bank officials stated
that the teller, who was an efficient employee, reported seeing the man in
front of her, and then immediately he vanished into thin air. She could
give no identification . . ."*

"And lissen to this part: . . . *when a police pressed the teller, she
immediately lost her power to speak and had to be taken in a city ambulance to a mental institution. Medical authorities say that this is extraordinary, though probably . . . police were reluctant to call it the perfect
robbery . . ."*

"Lemme *see* that."

"It here, in black-and-white, man! Christ, I wish you was that
bank-robber, but as I tell you, I couldn't see you pulling-off a
thing like that."

"Lemme see that paper . . ."

"That man with that twenty-thousand dollar bills is a real gorilliphant tonight!"

CHAPTER 18

Austin Clarke: Defying the Silence, a Life in Letters

John Harewood

"Don't do muh so!" I can hear Austin's voice issuing the repri-
mand, tongue in cheek, from his study as he looks through the
window on to Moss Park, which inspired *Where the Sun Shines
Best*, one of the last three books he published. Immediately afterwards, I can hear him adding, "God don't like ugly." Those of us
who knew him well might justifiably argue that he would have
reacted in this way on hearing the news that a special collection
was being published in his honour.

I was a junior to Austin at high school in the early fifties and,
like most of his contemporaries, admired his outstanding achievement as an athlete when he won the Victor Ludorum trophy for
two consecutive years. The idea of being a specialist just in one
or two races on the track simply didn't exist and Austin would in
later years look contemptuously at those athletes could perform
brilliantly in only one race and spent all of their time training for
the grand occasion.

I had seen him run, had witnessed the scene when he received
the trophy in one of his years of triumph, but I had never heard
him speak. Indeed, I had never heard his voice until he sang the
part of King John in the production of *1066 and All That* by
the Harrison College Dramatic Society in 1952.

You couldn't miss his rich baritone, resonant with a touch of huskiness as he crooned,

> I and Richard played as boys together
> Best of friends for many years were we
> I was always nervous as a kitten
> Richard lionhearted as could be
> Unlucky John, always sat upon,
> Unlucky John, je ne suis plus bon.

> Richard died, I took his crown and jewels
> Then, one day when I was forced to flee,
> I was washed into the wash at washpool
> Then I lost my washing in the sea.
> Unlucky John, all my clothes have gone,
> Unlucky John, I've got nothing on.

I am wondering now, whether in later years, he ever saw the last line as a metaphor for his life, that somehow he was often stripped and laid bare for all to see. And ironically, these recent efforts to celebrate him and his work, however justified, might appear to some of his admirers to be yet another stripping, if not an unmasking. For Austin, despite his very public persona, was a very private person.

He would have said that the first stripping had occurred before he entered Harrison College, when one of its cadet officers humiliated him by removing him from the rank of sergeant major as punishment for breaking camp. The next was administered by the headmaster of the same Harrison College, whose supposed "letter of recommendation" of him as a "transfer from Combermere" suggested that he had no real identity as an authentic college boy.

The feeling of rejection continued two years after his arrival in Canada in 1955. Not at all excited by the politics and economics program in which he had registered at Trinity College in the University of Toronto, he withdrew and, in quick succession, worked as a janitor, security guard, Christmas letter carrier, paint factory worker, sculptor, reporter, and stagehand. Tired of being fired, he decided to become a writer, vowing thereafter "not to work for a black or white boss."

Austin had grown up in a colonial setting where the presence of a foreign master, paradoxically, was both resented and courted. He had left that milieu when the emergence of a third force in world politics became apparent as formerly colonized peoples were asserting their right to self-determination and demanding a new international order based on human rights. In North America, especially the United States, that demand for change manifested itself in the civil rights movement. Canada was not immune to its influence and Austin was soon attracted.

He participated in the Canadian Apartheid Committee, boycotted South African goods, picketed Loblaw's supermarkets, wrote columns in the *Toronto Telegram* and *Toronto Star* protesting the company's hiring practices and blatant racism. Very quickly, he began to be described as an "activist," a word whose negative connotations more frequently cast its bearer as a troublemaker rather than an agent for positive change. So an article he wrote denouncing the discrimination that he had personally suffered between 1955 and the mid-sixties earned him the title of "Canada's Angriest Black Man" from *Maclean's* magazine.

I myself was among those Toronto Blacks who were uncertain as to whether we should be embarrassed or offended by his notoriety. We hailed the publication of his first novel, *The Survivors of the Crossing*, but thought that it wasn't about us, the experience we were living. Set in the Caribbean with Rufus as its dubious hero, whose desire for socio-economic change motivated his unsuccessful attempt to lead a rebellion against the established order of "the plantation," it still evoked some empathy, at least from those of us with Caribbean roots. It signalled the presence of a new voice. We could partly identify with it, but we weren't willing to accept its bearer as our leader or spokesman. We suspected that he had an alternative agenda.

With increased immigration from the Caribbean, Toronto's demography changed. However, these new immigrants weren't being reflected in the country's literature. Like Austin, they were invisible, although conspicuously present. No other writer was addressing their experience of displacement, racial discrimination, alienation, loneliness, or unemployment. He was determined to make them visible, to give them a voice, and emphasize the significance of their presence.

Except that there was no obvious model in the Canadian literary establishment, nor did he think that Dickens, Chaucer, Eliot, and Shakespeare—with whom he had grown up—could be imported to meet the challenge. Rather, he chose to describe the new social reality by introducing a new way of seeing, through a different lens and a language rich in the sounds, rhythms, colour, smells, and humour of the Caribbean. And so was born the now famous Toronto Trilogy: *The Meeting Point* (1967), *Storm of Fortune* (1973), and *The Bigger Light* (1975), featuring Dots, Bernice, and Boysie.

Under his pen, they are Black immigrants from the Caribbean, but nonetheless, they possess all of the aspirations common to any immigrant, as well as the determination to achieve their dreams despite the occasional racism they suffer because of the colour of their skin. Boysie is the prototype; he has achieved the goals pursued by every immigrant—job security and financial success. Yet, his enjoyment of his new status is jeopardized by an increasing alienation from his wife and the West Indian community, toward which he develops a troubling antipathy. This accounts for his constant uncertainty, his preoccupation with a world of fantasy, and a relentless search for "the bigger light."

I had seen Austin briefly on the street one day in 1964 when he informed me that he had published his first novel. I met him again shortly after *Storm of Fortune* appeared. My copy still bears his autograph with the words, "For John Harewood from the homeland with love, Toronto, 7 July, 1973." He had already persuaded me by letter, in his trademark style of calligraphy, to write for

Contrast, the Black community paper of the day. On October 23, 1972, he wrote:

> Harewood!
>
> Send some papers fuh we, nuh? And keep in touch, yuh hear. You want to review books for we? Well, ok, buy the kiss-me-arse book, then and write the review. We don't pay. I working free, so you understand!

This letter was the beginning of our forty-four years of correspondence and a very close friendship. If Clarke's memoirs and novels give a view of his public voice, his letters communicate another side. After all, here was a man who enjoyed a multi-faceted career, as writer, but also as a diplomat, politician, teacher, professor, and bureaucrat. In the letters, invariably, he is brutally frank, uninhibited, irreverent, and unapologetic, but at the same time charming, humorous, and empathetic. In general, Austin didn't assign titles to his letters, but he seems to have reserved his strongest opinions and most graphic and colourful language for certain topics, which I have tried to reflect in the excerpts that follow.

Love, Women, and Marriage

1:20 p.m. Wednesday, December 27, 2000,
I here, Harewood, on this nice bank holiday, listening to calypsos from the 1990s and really enjoying them. . . . But there is a reason that I so happy these days, Harewood. Woman. Harewood, when I tell you "woman," Harewood, um is the first time in my life, that I actually fall in love with a woman. . . . I mean a woman-and-a-half. I never knew love could be so sweet. Man, she have me doing things I never do before in my life. Things that sweet. Things that bring-out the man and that bring-out the woman. The things that true love made of. But more than anything is the peace that she bring into my life. Peace and security and sure-ness. And confidence.

Writing, Other Writers, and Friendship

March 26, 1974,

Man, if I had was to begin life all over again from the beginning, I would cram scientific phrases and be a kiss-me-arse psychiatriss. But to want to be a writer and nobody ain drive some blows in your clothes to mek you one, and you choose that by yourself, man that is suicide of self, man. Writing hard as shite. I just finding that out.

12:45 p.m. April 23, 1988,

And I uses to dream o' days when I too, couldda be in my barrister silks, and walk with a limp o' style, always pulling up my trousers, and looking as if I have in rums and talking pure big words and legal phraseologies . . . and hold over the railing and look down 'pon lesser mortals. . . . My dreams did always big dreams. And when I hit 'pon that idea in Proud Empires, at the very beginning o' the novel, I was real proud, and did in fact, to some degree, writing about my own-own fantasies.

11:06 a.m. January 9, 1997, while writing *The Origin of Waves*:

If you siddown beside a lake too often, and in particular 'pon a dark night, the only intellectual thing for you to do, is jump in the blasted lake, yuh! Suicide must come in your mind. Um is as if the water is the water you was contain in, when you was in your mother's womb, and now that you born, and is even a man, the realism of this lake is to suck you back In water, have a compelling force like it want to suck you back in. . . . So, in a sense, it isn't suicide in the normal sense, but a kind of enforce re-entry inside the womb.

I write the book, yuh! I write the book saying this, but didn't know what the arse I was saying when I write um. And continuing the metaphor, I see my life as a kiss-me-arse lake.

Regarding *More*, his last novel, he was more expansive:

The structure of this novel is different from all the rest I have written; and I am trying out a new idea of not making the narrative follow a line that

is straight, but one that stops abruptly and then may continue with a
flashback . . . and then reconnect with the beginning of the narrative. . . .
I have the same feeling of excitement writing this novel, as I had when I
was writing The Polished Hoe.

1:00 p.m. December 31, 1985,
Yesterday was a sad day for literature and people who work in
literature; Jack McClelland sold his firm; but as you may know by now,
he will remain the publisher for at least five years. All the big shots in the
whirl of literature were there at the Royal York, in the library room. And
once again, I had to say that it is a pity that I am the only black writer
who has that profile. . . . And I suspect that since there were so few of us
writers, Atwood, Gibson, Berton, and Templeton, invited to that important
and significant ceremony, that my stars must be pitching, at last.

2.57 p.m. February 27, 1981, when Andrew Salkey, "one of the
pioneers o' Wessindian Literature," once visited Toronto with Kamau
Brathwaite and Paule Marshall, Clarke was ecstatic:
Braff and Handrew Salkey and Paule Marshall, did here. Man, they get
on bad bad bad. Paule Marshall put a reading 'pon de people up at
York, that had them bawling fuh murder. And Braff read "Negus" from
Masks, with the thing that does go "it, it, it, it is not, it is not, it is not
enough to be semi-colon, semi-colony" and Jesus Christ, Harewood, I
telling you um was pure po'try and fire and brimstones and rockstones
he pelt- bout in that auditorium. Pretty pretty pretty fuh so! . . . Then,
Handrew Salkey face the new ball. . . . He slam Naipaul to the boundary
for selling out. Plam.

Miscellaneous Concerns

Clearly, he had reached a low point emotionally in the summer of
1996. At 2:19 p.m. on August 26, 1996, he wrote:
I have two dollars and twenty-something cents to my name. Um can't
buy coffee. Um can't buy a stamp. Um can't buy a butter-tart. Um
can't buy a return ticket 'pon the subway, in case I want to go down

by the lake and jump in; or, if I change my mind concerning the jumping in, crawl-back here. Um can't buy a beer not even a draff-beer. And um sure can't buy a pack o' cigarettes. . . . So, I have to wait and see if there is a God, and if he have any mercy 'pon writers. Sometimes, I don't think so. This is one Monday morning when I know-so.

All he had now, was memories, stories, tales of a past, much of the details of which he could not even be sure. But since his life had no string to it he amused himself not only by re-membering these clouds of dreams, but also by inventing & investing them with facts as he would have wanted those facts to have been. He found it difficult though to keep the string of his past continually in the memories which he invited to give his present the meaning he yearned for. Dreams were merely dreams with no reality & memories were not memories without the basis of a dream. He had nothing left of which he was proud proud enough of that he would want to risk the expenditure of energy in: nothing. But he was not without hope. There was no such desperation in him. His life which now was a mere whir of exited portions was not always in such disjointed repair. For he had lived once. Through four women each of whom he told himself would be the last: no one to follow the first - for he had not thought past that first experience. But with time, all four experiences faded into one. He was no longer concerned with the precise shape of things; & memories held no dimensions for him now. All he had now, was memories which were like clouds and the past that is not too pleasant that it is to be remembered so clearly that it revives the feelings encountered in that past of present living. That present past was lived in three distinct countries of borders & of language & of customs. He remembered the dimensions of the three countries better than the shape & the configuration of the four women. The four women were the outlines now

Austin Clarke diary entry.
Permissions: The Estate of Austin Clarke

And, in the summer of 1997, at the very moment when the first tribute to him was organized at Toronto's Harbourfront and he was thinking about attempting a new start in Italy, he wrote at 11:16 a.m. on July 21: *I feel like a new immigrand, just land, and facing this big city, not knowing where the next kiss-me-arse meal going come from. And all this realism in the midst of praise! . . . I can't even walk and lick-bout two brown pennies inside my fob-pocket. I asking myself, what this mean? I asking myself, I do somebody something, that God like he forget me? I asking myself, if I in the middle of a cycle o' blows, that have to run its revolution before I could come up for breath, before I drown? I asking myself, if this is the end? I asking myself, if I on the cusp or the crust o' something more bigger than me-myself?*

On meeting the Queen. 12:40 p.m. July 29, 2004,
Man, when I enter Buckennam that morning in March, the eighth at 12:40 p.m., the exact hour that I happen to address this letter to you . . . I never, in my wildest dreams thought that me and Her Majesty would one day, in Buckennam, shake hands; and that she would smile in my face and axe me, "And what tie are you wearing, Mr. Clarke?" When I tell she um was Harsun College, in Barbados, she eyes light up, and she tell me, "Oh yes! My trainer is a Barbadian, Stoute. I think his father was a Commissioner of Police in Barbados. . . . And that cause me to chirp-in and tell bout my step-father; bout 434 Luke driving the Commissioner car; bout Stoutie youngest brother being the Dean of my cathedral church . . . and thing and thing . . . and we end up like two old friends, discussing the advantages and multiple disadvantages of the computer. . . . Harewood, when I tell you that it was sweet, sweet, sweet, then . . .

On his lifelong love of cooking. 3:37 p.m., November 20, 2004,
You might very well become distraught when I tell you what I am doing at this time. I am sipping a cold, dry, very dry Bombay Sapphire martini, made by my own two hands, with a thick slice of the skin from a grapefruit; in a very chilled glass; and eating slices of French brie cheese.
And guess what? Don't kill me when I confess what I doing, in addition to sipping a Bombay Sapphire, and eating a little good cheese.

I cooking . . . Basmati rice and Jamaica red beans, boiled down in some juicy pig tails; with a gravy and a sauce of beef short ribs that I buy from the Sin-Lawrence Market; braizing in a gravy with red wine, onions, fresh tomato, Jamaican jerk seasoning, and the usual condiments. My God, Harewood, I too-glad you ain't here, so I have to share this "Bittle" with you, don't mind you is my best friend! Some things friendship can't come betwixt-and-between, and don't mind the "longtitude" and the "latitude" o' that friendship.

The Sessions

We called them sessions! Informal get-togethers! There might have been two of us, three of us, or four of us. A session was held in Toronto, at 62 McGill or 150 Shuter; in Ottawa, at Carl Taylor's, Gregg Edwards's, Charles Skeete's, or my place. A session might begin at the Grand Hotel, but, while that venue was highly favoured, it was really a warm-up. The real thing occurred at a house, at no fixed time, and it was understood that it could continue indefinitely. Only three components were predictable: conversation, food, and drink.

Sometimes, I would call ahead to let Austin know that I was coming to town or he would inform me, by letter, that he would be coming to Ottawa to be a part of the jury to select a winner for the Governor General's Award for fiction, or for some other assignment. Alternatively, I would call from Union Station when I arrived. If he happened to be at home, which was often the case, Austin would invite me to come over. His hospitality would start as soon as I entered the house. He would offer a beverage of choice or tea and something to eat. We would talk, perhaps about a current news story, what was happening in our lives, or what he was working on.

On occasion, I would stay overnight, bunking on the sofa on the second floor, amidst shelves of books with Miles Davis or John Coltrane on in the background, while Clarke sat working in his study until dawn, often preferring his faithful Bertha, an old IBM typewriter, to his laptop. Shortly after he returned from a reading trip to Australia in 2004, we met in the Grand Hotel, his watering hole. As usual, he was the last to leave and, to quote him, "We closed it."

We then retired to 150 Shuter and held session, sipping tea as he recalled the warm reception given to him by some white Bajans who had migrated "Down Under." He was pleasantly surprised by their familiarity with his work.

Morning broke, whereupon he suggested that we return to the Grand for breakfast, still clothed as we had been the previous evening. This was unusual, for after a session like that, he would normally prepare breakfast as he did once when I overnighted. I had come down to attend "Honouring Austin Clarke," an event organized by the Caribbean Consular Corps and the Caribbean Canadian Literary Expo at the Toronto Reference Library. On that occasion, he offered me his bedroom in the attic while he toiled through the night working on a short story.

I last saw him on November 1, 2015. The Toronto International Authors' Festival had included a tribute to him to coincide with the publication of 'Membering. He was too weak to attend, but after the proceedings, a number of us trooped over to 150 Shuter for a session. The protocol was familiar. Much to eat and drink. Lively conversation. He was quiet, sometimes amused, ever attentive.

I increased calling on my return to Ottawa but reached him only twice in the New Year. On the morning of June 27, 2016, his daughter, Darcy, called to let me know of his passing. She asked me to be one of the pallbearers.

8:09 a.m. January 12, 1996:
But Harewood!

And talking 'bout time, why am I at this early hour this morning spenning time 'pon you, you brute-beast who negleck me all them months when you was mekking hay in hay-loffs and haywoods and laughing? Because we is friends. And was friends from long. And, gorblummuh, going- remain likewise till I sing "The Day Thou Gavest"

over you or you sing The Day Thou Gavest over me, meaning till one
o' we dead. Or, in other words, lifelong friends.

"The Day Thou Gavest" was the second hymn at the funeral
service held for Austin Ardinel Chesterfield "Tom" Clarke at the
Cathedral Church of St. James in Toronto, on Friday, July 8, 2016.

I sat behind Loretta and Darcy, and beside Jordan and her
husband. I sang.

CHAPTER 19

Austin Clarke Love Poem

Cyril Dabydeen

For J.H.

"Woman," Harewood, when I tell you *woman*,
Harewood, um is the first time in my life
I actually fall in love with a woman,
I mean a woman-and-a-half—
I never knew love could be so sweet.
Man, she have me doing things
I never do before in my life,
things that sweet—
things that bring-out the man,
things that bring-out the woman,
things that true love made of,
but more than anything
is the peace that she bring
into my life. Peace and security
and sure-ness. And confidence.

CHAPTER 20

Do Not Let Them Choose the Fragrance

Austin Clarke

In the summer of 1979 Albert Johnson, a Jamaican immigrant, was shot dead by the Toronto police in his home on a Sunday morning. Johnson was alleged to have been holding an axe; the axe was, in fact, a lawn edger. Johnson's murder and the high-profile police trial that followed (both officers were acquitted) became a rallying point for the Black community in Toronto and across Canada. Albert Johnson's legacy pervades Clarke's writing: his characters regularly dream, remember, and share stories of the fate of "poor Mr. Albert Johnson." In this poem, written in 1979, Clarke responds to this outrageous police violence by directly addressing Albert and Lemona Johnson's children. Clarke calls on the subsequent generations, who must bear the burden of witnessing this collective pain, to not surrender the beauty and hopefulness of vision that is their true inheritance.

For the children of Mrs. Lemona Johnson

Do not let *them* choose the fragrance
for your lives and the beauty
In the flowers that you hold to kiss.
Their roses are made from plasticine.

And do not change the diet of your righteousness;
rice and peas are yours: theirs is bloodied steak.
Do not let them turn the pages of your book:
Bible, poetry or dogma, with their cold hand.
Ras Tafari, drums and Allah are your
beating heart. Theirs is board; in crisis, and
Timetabled hard against you. Do not, *do not*
let *them* come again into your yard,
Incensed with religion, their evil excuse,
dictator and belching Sunday missionaries, who
Rip the pawned Bible their grandfathers gave
to make your father kneel as if he'd say
A prayer. Prayers in this policing world are
answered with spit, with billy clubs
With cold white bullets spewing from
indecent thighs. Do not, *do not* let them
Make your father bend his knee to that religion, and
surrender his sanity to their white wards.
You are the black, sane surviving witnesses
to their madness. Do not, do not let
Them forget their white Sunday: fix the images,
garden tool and revolver in the hand of your
Brain, and let that be the text of your immigration.
But, do not let *them* clip the flowers for your
Nostrils. Your fragrance cleanse their gas. You must
remember. Do not forget that "them killed
Your father." Face the cold word of their murder!
and do not let them suck your young fragrance.
Marley, Marcus, Manley and McMurtry—givens, among
Babylonian petals in your eyes;
But *do not let them* blind your fragrance.

CHAPTER 21

There Will Never Be Another Austin Clarke

Patrick Crean

Patrick Crean is one of Canadian literature's best-known and most respected editors. From his beginnings monitoring the slush pile at McClelland and Stewart, he has gone on to edit and publish a number of award-winning novels, including three Giller Prize winners: Esi Edugyan's Half-Blood Blues *and* Washington Black *and Austin Clarke's* The Polished Hoe. *His relationship with Clarke stretches back to the 1970s, when he edited* The Prime Minister, *and Crean has had a lengthy professional and personal relationship with Clarke. On a Bloor Street patio during the summer of 2019, Paul Barrett and Patrick Crean sat down to discuss editing Austin Clarke.*

Clarke's Black Power Conservatism

I first met Austin in 1976 when I was living on Brunswick Avenue in Toronto and Austin and his family lived just north of me, near Jan Sibelius Park. My first wife loved jazz and used to hang out at the First Floor Club, had met Austin, and eventually hooked us up. This was when I was with General Publishing, the forerunner of the Stoddart imprint and we signed Austin to write *The Prime Minister*. I remember it was during the Black Power era and he was, of course, involved in that with his activism, appearing on television and, among other things, interviewing Malcolm X in New York for the CBC.

There was some sense of that in the book: a kind of Black Power satire of Caribbean politics. Part of the plot of *The Prime Minister* came out of Austin's appointment as the head of the Caribbean Broadcasting Corporation. His tenure was not only short but from what he told me, actually dangerous; he spoke out against corruption and he was pretty disliked at that time on the island and there was talk of guns. This feeling made it into *The Prime Minister* and it led to the book being banned in Barbados until quite recently.

This was my first introduction to Austin. I was twenty-six at the time, working with this Black intellectual who was, in many ways, terrifying to be around because he would drop into these silences and just smoke his pipe and stare for long minutes, sometimes even an hour, wordlessly contemplating my edits, or just sitting with me wordlessly. Once he sat for an entire hour in silence over lunch at the Park Plaza because he felt he was not getting enough publicity for his book. He was like an African king. Imperial. Imperious.

There was this paradoxical sense in everything that Austin did. Was he a progressive or a conservative? He spent some time working for the Ontario Board of Censors. But he also worked for the Immigration and Refugee Board of Canada after that. Then there was the launch for *The Prime Minister* at the Underground Railroad restaurant, which was attended by a number of Progressive Conservative politicians: Bill Davis, Roy McMurtry, and a number of other members of the Ontario PC Party. That was Austin: Conservative politicians attending his book launch alongside members of the Black Power community. Austin ran for a Conservative nomination (and didn't get it) and also wrote for the Black newspapers; he might have even liked Margaret Thatcher! I could always imagine Austin in the House of Commons in a Churchillian manner. He was an incredibly articulate and eloquent public speaker with his slow Barbadian cadence. But still: Who was he? What were his politics? Where did he really fit?

That was also my first introduction to the challenge of selling Black literature in a predominantly white Canada, and Austin's work more generally. I think today his work is neglected and overlooked. And yet, I am certain he must be an influence on today's Black writers. I am sure there was inspiration there for Dionne Brand, Lawrence Hill, or Esi Edugyan and others. He is the grandfather of Black Canadian letters. Can you think of anyone before him?

After *The Prime Minister* we had something of a breakup and didn't work together again for over twenty years. Austin moved around to a number of publishers and by all accounts was notoriously hard to work with. At the same time, though, the celebrated publisher Jack McClelland is quoted as saying that "Austin is one of our greats." I think Austin drove everyone crazy at M&S, but Jack really thought very highly of his writing and talent.

We really didn't have any contact in the years after *The Prime Minister* but in the very early 2000s we got back together. His agent had gotten into some kind of dispute with McClelland and Stewart and Austin felt that he couldn't work with M&S any longer. So he approached me, completely out of the blue, and said, I've got this book, would you be interested? It was called *The Polished Hoe*.

Editing *The Polished Hoe*

I was just starting out with this brand new imprint, the opportunity of my career, at Thomas Allen. The first thing you worry about with a new imprint is credibilty: so getting Austin on board was an absolute gift. Because of his already considerable literary reputation, he was our ticket to getting some publishing cred. So we began to work on *The Polished Hoe*. And what he first delivered to me was a gigantic, enormous, huge manuscript, over fifteen hundred pages. It was one of the most fascinating and challenging edits I've ever done.

I was lucky because I was able to head up north with that manuscript and repair to an island in Georgian Bay, by myself, for ten days. There was no electricity, no television, no Internet, so the quality of my attention was exceptionally focused; I lived with this novel for ten solid days with no interruption in complete solitude.

I remember to this day reading into the manuscript on that island and saying aloud to myself: "Holy fuck! This is a masterpiece!" The hairs were going up on my neck. It happened during

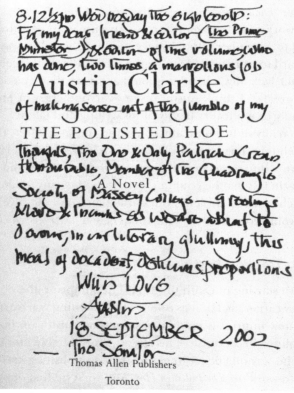

Patrick Crean's copy of *The Polished Hoe* with dedication from Austin Clarke.

Permissions: Patrick Crean

one of the scenes in the book about the hurricane and as I was reading this, I just *knew* it was a masterpiece. I can remember that vividly. The feeling is still with me.

Yet, despite that feeling, the manuscript was uneven and terribly lumpy, repetitive, and at times overwrought. It was a huge, glorious mess. So I was up there for ten days, isolated and editing, working intensely to turn this giant pile of paper into something that hung together: making notes, and crossing out entire pages and sections. It helped that he wrote triple spaced with huge margins that invited you to *really* edit it.

I must add a lovely detail here: Austin had a beautiful and distinct hand. He wrote with an ink fountain pen and his notes would fill the triple space; sometimes with comments; sometimes with revisions. We would write back and forth that way, as well as me giving him a general editorial note.

When I returned to Toronto, we met at Massey College, and he just stared at me in that familiar, silent way. Austin could read body language as well as he could read the editorial notes; he had an incredible sense of intuition around his craft. I know this sounds completely counterintuitive, but when we met he would pick up on what was wrong with the narrative without even looking at my notes. In that respect he was actually quite wonderful to work with—of course there were challenges, but he was such a pro. He didn't go off and grumble; well, he might sulk a bit, but in the end he would understand that there was work to be done. That was the situation with *The Polished Hoe.* I remember sitting down at Massey College with him, praising the manuscript, but also reporting on my first round of edits and the work ahead. So he left, taking the manuscript with him.

Then the manuscript came back from Austin. He had put back all of the parts I had cut out! We went back and forth with this two or three times. Finally, he agreed that maybe I had a point and reinstated most of the cuts. For me, this was as much a matter of wrestling with the author as it was about my job representing the reader. When one is lost in the narrative, because things have gotten too abstract, or the plot is too complicated, the challenge is to pull it all together in some coherent manner, while at the same time making sure the author has realized his intent—and not imposing oneself on the narrative.

I will admit, though, that when I worked with Austin I did worry about a white editor editing a Black sensibility. And I don't mean just the content of the narrative, but more the tonality of his prose and what I think of as the music of that book: there are subtle layers of African-American and Caribbean rhythms in *The Polished Hoe*. You need to listen carefully. I have always loved jazz. And reading Austin is reading jazz. So what I try to do as an editor is to approach text as though it is musical score. In my first reading, I'm not using my intellect as much as I am listening; I want to allow the text to work on me through its rhythms. And that really required great delicacy and attention because this is not my culture. I have to admit that he really startled me once when he said in jest after a particularly intense edit that I was a damn slave-driver!

There were really only two major disagreements about the editing of the book. The first concern I had was about the character of Bellfeels, the cruel plantation owner. In the early drafts of the novel Bellfeels was too *singularly* evil. I insisted that I didn't think he could write a character that evil and be believable on the page. So Austin allowed that Bellfeels needed some more complexity as a character.

The second concern, and perhaps the strangest part of that editing process, was our disagreement over the ending of the book. We were engaged in that struggle right up to the deadline. Weeks before the book was set to go to the printer, Austin was insisting that the book should end with Sargeant raping Mary-Mathilda.

I completely disagreed; I said, "Austin, that's totally out of character. It doesn't work, it comes out of nowhere, it would simply kill the book." There's no doubt, of course, that Sargeant had a crush on Mary Mathilda, and I could imagine him coming onto her or kissing her, but violently so? Raping her? For me, it simply didn't ring true given how these characters behaved throughout the the novel. Thankfully, Austin came around to see my perspective.

On *The Polished Hoe* Being Shortlisted for the Giller

When the book went off to the critics, the reviews were spectacular: he'd hit a home run. Then we were all gobsmacked when the book was shortlisted for the Giller. There was no longlist in those days; he was just immediately shortlisted.

Part of my surprise was that in spite of the inherent brilliance of the novel, Clarke's writing can be really challenging; *The Polished Hoe* was a polarizing and challenging book: it takes place in one night; it has a Joycean movement to it. It is circular, subterranean, subtle, and works on many levels, but is the kind of novel that rewards the more you work at it. The other part of the surprise seeing him get shortlisted for the Giller is that Austin's work had to that point been somewhat overlooked. That was partially because of the complexity of the work and partially because he wasn't exactly the most popular person in the world. He had alienated too many people in his life. Of course, a lot of great writers are ignored or not recognized, but this was made more acute because race played a significant role in the reception of Austin's writing.

Austin, very wisely, said at our Giller gala table beforehand: "Whatever happens tonight, there shall be no tears." The tension in that room was intense, and when he won it was absolutely incredible. When his name was announced, and they said, "The winner of the 2002 Giller Prize is Austin Clarke," there was an audible intake of breath in the room and this undercurrent of "Woah, how could this be?" We, of course, were thrilled; but everyone in the room thought the winner was going to be Carol Shields—she was dying of cancer—and the audience wasn't prepared for Austin to win. Carol Shields was definitely the popular choice that year.

When he won it was, of course, fantastic, but also a little bit bittersweet and odd because Austin delivered a bold speech that was eloquent, but it was also aggressive and even gloating. He talked about conquering and looting; there was a sense of "I have won" and "Here I am, a Black man in a sea of white faces." It was certainly a moment of triumph for him. Once again, he broke the mould.

Winning the Giller was a career-changing moment. He had money, he did a huge renovation on his house, he celebrated, he was a king in a castle. During that Giller glow of a year or two, we were really rocking. We both thanked each other for what we'd done for one another. He was generous with me and acknowledged his editor publically, the amount of work that had gone into the writing and editing. We were compadres. At the same time, I'm not sure he behaved terribly well: Austin became *orgueilleux*, he became arrogant, so it made things difficult in that way too.

After the Giller he had said to the press that he was one of the few writers in Canada who could live off his earnings. This *was* true, but it rapidly became untrue. He *really* celebrated his win and while he certainly made good money from *The Polished Hoe*, it didn't last forever.

That's one of the sad things about writing in Canada. When André Alexis accepted his Giller, he said, "Now I'm even." The win simply pulled him out of debt and brought his balance *up* to zero. Michael Redhill said he had five dollars in his bank account the day before winning. That's simply the state of things in Canada. Austin, of course, relished his victory and his accolades, but eventually it came time to get back to work.

Visiting Barbados

I had some insight into Austin's life when, just after *The Polished Hoe* had come out, I had the good fortune to visit Barbados and stay with friends. My wife, the novelist Susan Swan, and I visited Austin's childhood neighbourhood: we went to St. Matthias

Church, where he had gone to Sunday services with his mother, and we went to Harrison College to sit on the benches in the Great Hall. It may seem obvious, but the journey this man took from real poverty to celebrating his victory at the Gillers is pretty incredible. I was so struck by this: he went from poverty to the equivalent of Upper Canada College in Barbados to the University of Toronto to winning the Giller Prize. He was very proud of that.

As much as Austin writes about race, he's also writing about class. And if you think about it, in Canadian literature, how many working class writers do we really have? The Canadian literary community can be quite an insular establishment along both racial and class lines. Perhaps that also had something to do with his sense of alienation?

I mean, he wore his Harrison College jacket when he went to meet the Queen. That was certainly one of the highlights of his career. He told me that he would ask her for a pardon for having a written a book entitled *Growing Up Stupid Under the Union Jack*. But apparently they had a good chat, they both knew someone in common in Barbados.

To understand Austin's perspective, we have to think of him arriving here, in the middle of winter in the 1950s, to attend Trinity College in a very white and pretty racist society. Without a shadow of a doubt, Austin Clarke broke the mould in this country, I mean in particular the white domination of creative writing.

Austin was raised with dignity and pride in what is mostly a homogenous Black society of Barbados, then arrives in Canada, and finds himself in a prejudiced and somewhat backwater Canadian culture that's only beginning to find itself. He would tell me about the racism he experienced—the question he would get asked again and again: "Who do you think you are?" He would try to do basic things like change his train ticket and they'd give him a hard time. Simply because he was Black.

We see this continuing today. But now more Black writers are pushing back, raising awareness and fighting racism. For example, with Esi Edugyan's *Washington Black*, in some respects she's taking on white people who are sympathetic to Black people but in fact are more concerned about the moral stain on themselves than they are about the condition of Black people. For so many white people the response to racism is "I'm so sorry, but I'm a progressive, I'm not at all racist; I'm a liberal." Austin then, and Esi now, among other Black writers, are showing the limitations of that white, liberal perspective.

On Publishing *More*

After celebrating the Giller for some time, I began to ask him about his next work. He had been talking about this novel *More* that he'd worked on for years and was hoping to return to. In the 1970s he had embarked on a version of the novel, about a woman who had worked for a Jewish family in Forest Hill. Austin always had a bitterness and anger toward Forest Hill and rich Jewish people.

When *More* came to me it was an unfinished novel that centred on the Domestic Scheme, which he was, of course, very taken up with. This is the program that was arranged between the Canadian government and governments in the West Indies that has come under heavy criticism for being the next thing to slave labour.

So what started as something of a reflection on the relationship between Black people in Toronto and rich Jewish families in Forest Hill became more of a meditation on Black oppression in Canada alongside the experience of generational disconnect. *More* was an urban, Canadian novel as opposed to the wider canvas of *The Polished Hoe*, which we can see as a metaphor for the broader history of slavery in the Caribbean.

I will say that, at the height of his powers, Austin was a world-beater. He was an extraordinary writer when he was in top form. But *More*, in some ways, reflects a decline in his powers. That said, this may have to do with its lengthy publication history. *More* was something else back in the early drafts in the 1970s, and it morphed into what it is now.

The beginning of *More* required a huge line edit: he and I really wrestled over the first half of the book. The prose was weaker than *The Polished Hoe* and it didn't have the same tensility or robustness. When it was released, I remember feeling hopeful when he was longlisted for the Giller and then dashed when he didn't get shortlisted. Yet now when I reflect on it, while I do think it is a good novel, it certainly isn't a masterpiece. It did, however, win the Toronto Book Award that year.

Nevertheless, Austin's decline continued in his later years and then I turned down some material that really was not publishable. This affected our relationship at the end of his life; particularly so because his powers were fading. He was working on a final novel called *So What?* after the Miles Davis piece, and it just didn't work. As an editor, I think there's an underlying quality of life experience (or not) that imbues a writer's line: the wisdom, life experience, and maturity (or lack thereof) of that particular artist arising from his or her unconscious. Austin's later work had a very muddy and disconnected quality.

At the very end, he asked me to look at some new short stories. But they were simply not good enough—and I could not see how any amount of work and editing could improve them—and I turned them down. They did not have the power of his earlier work. He took my rejection of those stories very personally and felt that I'd betrayed him—but sadly, the fact was these stories were just not up to the quality of his previous work.

Our relationship really suffered because of this: I had also commissioned him to write a memoir (*'Membering*) but the draft was so abstract and vague and with so much disconnected riffing on various topics that I couldn't imagine many people being interested in it. Instead of writing clearly and honestly about his life, he chose innuendo, obscure code, abstraction, vagueness, and a meandering potpourri of half-baked memories.

But when a not dissimilar text that puported to be a memoir finally came out with another press what really struck me was the extent to which he was truly the unreliable narrator of his own life. It wasn't just his characters, Idora and Mary-Mathilda, but Austin himself who was paradoxical and unreliable. It was quite astonishing how he could make up things about his own life or avoid difficult truths.

On Their Friendship

In spite of all this, there was great fondness between us. I loved the man; I still love him. He certainly pissed me off at times. He made me very angry. But there was also something I loved about him. He'd come to my house on Brunswick, and he'd be so comfortable hanging out there. We'd go and have dinner together and he'd confide in me about everything happening with him. His loves, his concerns, his hopes and dreams.

Even though Austin could be a rascal, engaged in all kinds of misbehaviour toward his friends and family, I still had time for him I think because of those heady, exciting literary and publishing moments we shared. I was very honoured to be one of the pallbearers at his funeral, celebrating his life at the same church that he wrote about in *More*.

And yet, I felt sad at the end because it seemed that he was signalling he was disappointed in me. Sure, I thought he was being unfair, but he expected that I'd publish anything that he produced and that was unreasonable. His decline was very sad to witness.

But what I want to remember are those moments like the one on the island in Georgian Bay with Austin's masterpiece and the language and music of the text and the hurricane wafting over me: in that moment, I felt tremendously excited. If an editor has the luck to be able to work on a book like that, you can get this crazy feeling that impels you to want to run out on the street and tell everybody about how good the book is. Austin really was blessed as a great writer, able to conjure and produce brilliant material. I consider myself exceptionally lucky to have known him and to have had a working relationship, as well as a friendship, with him. There certainly will never be another Austin Clarke. As Man!

CHAPTER 22

Still the British Empire

André Forget

On September 29, 1955—a full decade before Northrop Frye likened the experience of entering Canada by ship to being swallowed whole by a vast continent—Austin Clarke flew into Montreal's Dorval Airport from Bridgetown, Barbados. Though he was carrying a letter of acceptance from McGill University, he was so unnerved by the treatment he received at the hands of the French-Canadian immigration personnel that he decided to keep going. By a stroke of luck, the clerk who had written out his ticket back in Barbados had accidentally extended his flight's terminus to Toronto.

At the time, it must have seemed like it didn't much matter: he had also received an acceptance letter from the University of Toronto. But writing in an old brick house on Shuter Street across from Moss Park fifty years later, Clarke remembered this day as one that "marked the change in my life which cannot be altered now; and in some cases, be redeemed" (*'Membering* 17).

This incident may have marked a change that would set the course of Clarke's sixty years in Canada, but it remains unmarked and unremarked upon in the literary history of this country. French philosopher Ernest Renan argues that "Forgetting . . . is an essential factor in the creation of a nation" because national "unity is always brutally established" (3). Just as the French-Canadian immigration official forgets the long history of Black presences in Canada, Clarke's work is routinely and willfully forgotten in Canadian literature.

This legacy of forgetting is most recently enacted in Nick Mount's *Arrival: The Story of CanLit* (2017), a study of Canadian literature during its boom years in the 1960s and '70s. Based on years of research and interviews with some of the period's most important figures, Mount's book purports to be the first full-length study of this remarkable and formative moment in Canadian letters. And yet the arrival of Clarke, who later came to be considered "Canada's first multicultural writer," is barely mentioned at all (*National Post* 2016). Mount's neglect of Clarke (he is cited only thrice in Mount's text) is not *only* exemplary of the larger problems with Mount's book, it is also illustrative of the literary establishment's ongoing failure to grant Black writers their place, and as such illuminates the paradoxes that underlie the construction of CanLit. Clarke was a fixture of Toronto's literary and cultural scene throughout the period chronicled in the pages of *Arrival.* When the CanLit boom was taking off, Austin Clarke wasn't just the most prominent Black writer in Canada: he was one of Canada's most prominent men of letters, period.

But Clarke was never only a Canadian, and the trajectory of his long and peripatetic career, moving from the West Indies to Canada and later to Britain, America, and Europe, challenges the very idea of a national literature. While Toronto might have been where he spent most of his life, his imagination was never constrained by national borders. As he wrote toward the end of his life, "I think of the most foreign and unusual cities, as home. Havana. Toronto. Venice. Manchester. Bordeaux. Toulouse. Amsterdam. Paris" (*'Membering* 257). The novel that won him the Giller Prize in 2002, *The Polished Hoe,* is set almost entirely in Barbados, and treats the complex and gothic colonial history of that nation at length; his virtuosic 2015 memoir *'Membering* devotes hundreds of pages to his years in the United States and Bridgetown; and his Toronto books are always meticulous about detailing the city's dazzling array of cultural and ethnic diversity, a diversity that he often explicitly ties to its imperial past, and neo-colonial present.

In doing so, Clarke played a foundational role in setting the terms for many of the debates about Blackness, marginalization, and migration that challenge received notions of Canadian literature. But his novels, essays, short stories, poems, and memoirs—some of which stand among the most innovative, challenging, and stylistically rich works of literature ever produced in this country—remind his readers that, however isolated and inward-looking it may be at times, Canada and the colonial governments that preceded it have always been an intimate participants in the violent movements of people, goods, capital, and ideas that produced and were produced by empire.

In his attention to particular experiences of Blackness, Clarke accesses a deep imperial history that predates the Commonwealth, Confederation, and even the American Revolution. In doing so, he celebrates the myriad ways Black people have resisted and continue to resist imperialism and colonialism. Clarke's engagement with the long history of Black life in the Caribbean, Europe, and North America illuminates the way that Black experiences have given rise to new political and aesthetic philosophies—philosophies that do not simply respond to imperialism and colonialism, but create new possibilities for imagining Blackness. His books conjure a morally complicated cosmopolitanism that serves as a corrective to the shallow liberal nationalism underpinning much popular thinking about Canada, a country constantly working to forget its own violent past.

The Second Elizabethan Era

As he recalled in his acerbically titled *Growing Up Stupid Under the Union Jack,* Clarke's education had indoctrinated him in the belief that as a subject of Her Majesty, he and his fellow Barbadians had a proud place in the family of imperial possessions: "We were English. We were the English of Little England. Little Black

Englishmen" (56). Through his education, he was "trained to be a snob, coached to be discriminating" (56). With his private school education, strong academic record, and deep immersion in the classics, the scriptures, and the English canon, Clarke was sure he would be able to succeed. He was a son of the British Empire, after all, and Canada was a branch in the family tree. Upon arriving in Canada, however, he would learn all too well how double-edged his colonial education had been.

After enrolling in the University of Toronto's Trinity College, Clarke became increasingly aware of how his Blackness intersected with racial, class, and gender hierarchies. The more Clarke saw of life in Toronto, the more it became apparent to him that for many white Canadians, his racial difference was far more significant than the education, literary tastes, and religious background he shared with them. And while he would become famous for his nuanced and sensitive portraits of the particularities of West Indian life in Toronto, his novels and stories always demonstrated a deep awareness that Canadians and West Indians were, in complicated, violent, and unequal ways, products of a shared history.

We see this very clearly in "An Easter Carol" and "They Heard a Ringing of Bells," the two pieces that open Clarke's first collection of stories, *When He Was Free and Young and He Used to Wear Silks* (1971). In and of itself, "An Easter Carol" is moving for its depiction of a simple matter that is not nearly as simple as it looks: the boy's short walk to the cathedral in uncomfortable shoes is, in the great tradition of Joycean realism, a window onto a whole way of life. Like Joyce, Clarke builds toward an epiphany that is also a disillusionment: the boy must wear shoes that do not fit because he must look his best, for his mother is proud of his role in the service. We understand that her desire for her son to succeed in the world of the cathedral is a desire for him to have a life that will distance him from her own emotional world. As he struggles in vain to put his shoes on even as his choral rival takes his place for the solo and the story reaches its crescendo, we are left with a certain ambiguity: in letting his mother down, has he been symbolically locked out of paradise, denied a chance at a better life? Or does he share in her reluctance to embrace the restrictions that come with the aspirational world of the cathedral?

That this is also a story about music is in no way incidental. The narrator, arriving at the cathedral, describes it as "facing me like my mother, unapproving" (Clarke is exceptionally good at this kind of angular word choice: the cathedral does not *disapprove* of him, it is indifferent), but when the bells start ringing they "filled my heart with joy" (13). The cathedral is not straightforwardly a good or bad place: it is a place where beautiful music is made, but where the congregation is left "dumb and washed-out by the sermon" (13). Clarke's attentiveness to the way buildings, objects, and brand names are both sources of everyday comfort and belonging and also visible signs of world-historical power is one of the most underappreciated elements of his fiction; cathedrals reoccur throughout as importantly ambivalent spaces. What building in Toronto is more symbolically loaded for *More*'s Idora Morrison than St. James Cathedral, a building that is made present most powerfully through the music of its bells?

Turning to the second story, we are immersed in music again. At the beginning of "They Heard a Ringing of Bells," West Indian expatriates Estelle, Ironhorse Henry, and Sagaboy are sitting on a campus lawn thousands of kilometres from the Islands, listening to what at first seems to be a very different set of bells. Estelle, who is from Barbados and has learned that she will be deported in a week, describes her tenuous new home as being "a different, but a more better, more advance place than where I come from" (17). But as the music continues, Estelle realizes that the hymn being played is "The Day Thou Gavest Lord Is Ending," the same hymn played at her drowned father's funeral. The music transports her, leading her to tell the story of the funeral, and how she believes her father had tried to speak to her as he was being buried. "Ain't it wondrous strange how a person remembers things that happen so long ago? And ain't it strange too, how a simple thing like a bell in a tower could cause that same person to travel miles and miles in memory?" (23).

Clarke's master stroke is to heighten the feeling of alienation central to these characters lives by emphasizing familiarity rather than difference. "You know something? I just realize that Sunday evening is the same all over the blasted world." Ironhorse Henry reminds his friends later on in the story. "We sitting down here in Canada, pon the grass, and it is the same thing as when we was little boys back home, sitting down in a place we used to call The Hill" (27). This colonial link is made explicitly in a bitter outburst from Sagaboy:

> I laugh hard hard as hell, hee-hee-hee! at all them people who say we shouldn't make Great Britain more blacker than she is or was, in the first Elizabethan era. And all the time I does be laughing, I does be thinking of long long ago when the Queen o' Britain send all them convicts and whores and swivilitic men and women overseas, to *fluck-up* and populate the islands! Well, darling, now the tables turn round, because this is the *second* Elizabethan era! And it is the islands who sending black people, *all kinds*, the good and the bad, the godly and the ungodly, and we intend to fuck-up the good old Mother Country. (19)

The relationship between the West Indians and Toronto is precisely *not* a relationship of difference or otherness: they are less strangers in a strange land than visiting relatives from a distant branch of the family, one that is maligned and distrusted for having been, for so long, mistreated.

From the very start of his writing career, Clarke was alive to this distinction. Born in a colony, he was sensitive to the fact that independent nations are never formed from whole cloth. When Canadians were forging a new literary identity for themselves in the 1960s and '70s by celebrating the pioneering past and enshrining the false myth of an empty continent, Clarke, the resident without citizenship, was busily outlining a new map of the world using the threads of Black experience. At the very moment when Canadian literary nationalism was reaching its apogee, Clarke's stories were laying the groundwork for a more skeptical, more cosmopolitan, and more formally inventive tradition of writing in Canada.

Nationalism and Empire

Clarke's journey toward becoming a novelist began in earnest in 1959, when he took a job as a feature writer for the *Timmins Daily News* in Northern Ontario. His work at the *Daily News* (and later at the *Globe and Mail*, after he returned to Toronto the next year) gave him an acute sense for the ordinary lives of Canadians along with some of the practical tools of the writer's trade. When he was fired from the *Globe* for writing a feature essay that was critical of the British high commissioner to Canada, Clarke dove headlong into fiction, turning out a remarkable five stories in just two weeks.

From his base at 46 Asquith Avenue he completed a manuscript for a novel, *The Love and the Circumstance*, and began work on what would become *The Meeting Point*. Despite his gruelling self-discipline and the stacks of pages flying out of his typewriter, concrete success eluded Clarke. In 1962, when he submitted a third manuscript, *The Trumpet at His Lips*, for consideration by McClelland and Stewart, it was turned down. By the end of that year, he had become convinced that if he were just to take a year to focus purely on his writing, he would have his breakthrough. This proved to be a fateful decision.

He spent 1963 writing what would become his first novel, *The Survivors of the Crossing*, published to positive reviews in 1964. A tragicomic account of a Barbadian plantation worker named Rufus who suffers emasculation, violence, and imprisonment for his attempts to organize a strike, *Survivors* explores the experiences of colonialism and dispossession in Barbados, borrowing from Clarke's own experience and—as he acknowledged in his

memoir—from the literature of Black America he found so inspiring. From the very beginning, Clarke's novels laid claim to a kind
of cosmopolitan Blackness, internationally inflected, honest to his
roots, and completely at odds with mainstream Canadian writing.
As 1964 stretched into 1965, 1966, 1967, his interest in diasporic culture and politics only deepened, and he continued to
involve himself in anti-racist activism in Toronto (much of it
alongside his Jewish ally, Rabbi Feinberg). His writing in this period is remarkable for its vivid, even febrile language, and for its
uncompromising indictment of systemic anti-Black prejudice.
He was also constantly travelling throughout these years: interviewing Malcolm X and Stokely Carmichael in New York, interviewing Derek Walcott back home in Barbados, visiting London
for a piece on West Indian migrants and Halifax's Africville to
interview Black Canadians, and publishing other in-depth interviews with Roy Innis, Chinua Achebe, and LeRoi Jones. He also,
somehow, found time to found the Ebo Society, a West Indian
cultural and advocacy group, and its (short-lived) print organ the
Ebo Voice, which would garner him the attention of Robin Winks,
a Yale historian working on a history of Black people in Canada.

Winks invited Clarke to Yale as a guest lecturer and then as a
visiting professor in the Department of African-American Studies
for the 1968–9 academic year. Clarke then spent the next three years
in a variety of different visiting lectureships and professorships at
several American colleges and universities. Indeed, Clarke's role in
establishing Black studies programs across the United States (and
giving Henry Louis Gates his only B+) is another under-studied
dimension of his career. These experiences placed him in the caul-
dron of American political debate at precisely the moment when
the Black Power movement was at its height, and, perhaps ironically, it left him with a grudging appreciation for Canada. Despite
his immersion in African-American culture and life, he always felt
like an outsider to Black American culture, which left him with a
lasting distaste for a country where he felt he could "only be a spec-
tator . . . even among my own people!" (Algoo-Baksh 94).

Meanwhile, in Canada, prominent Canadian writers like Graeme Gibson, Al Purdy, Gwendolyn MacEwen, Milton Acorn, Dave Godfrey, and Dennis Lee were vociferously protesting the slightest whiff of American cultural imperialism (Mount 190). A writer like Clarke, who had spent the decade studying Black history and uncovering the ties of migration, suffering, and rebellion that tied Black people to each other in England and Guyana, Bridgetown and Toronto, Halifax and New York, was distinctly out of step with the inward-looking, parochial, and overwhelmingly white concerns of the writers who were self-consciously building what would become CanLit. Certainly, Clarke's insistence on drawing attention to the connections between racism in Canada, the West Indies, and America to the great original sin of the transatlantic slave trade did little to endear him to white Canada.

But while there can be no doubt that this attempt to silence Clarke and downplay his prolific contributions to Canadian letters in the 1960s and '70s was racist, the particular quality of this racism is worth exploring: Clarke was not *only* rejected for being the "Angriest Black Man in Canada."[1] He was also rejected because his intellectual project, a cataloguing of Black experiences across the Caribbean and the wider Atlantic world, was an existential threat to a country that was trying to launder its colonial past and present itself to the world as a new kind of nation, free of Europe's historical sins and the institutionalized racial prejudices of the United States.

Here Is Where?

Clarke's attention to Canada's place in what Paul Gilroy calls "the black Atlantic" found its fullest expression in his literary style. In the introduction to this collection, Paul Barrett notes that Clarke's style is "both a reflection of his own particular artistic vision as well as a response to the erasure and absence of spaces for Blackness in Canada." He notes that Clarke uses style "to provoke, anger, baffle, annoy, and entertain." It is also, he argues, a "rebuke" to a Canadian literary establishment that so frequently "misread his work, treating it as a realist or sociological *account* of Black life in Canada."

This strategic use of style is present even in Clarke's earliest stories: by capturing the rhythm, syntax, and lexicon of nation language, on the page, Clarke did more than simply provide a realistic representation of how people spoke. But Clarke's use of nation language is only one aspect of the innovative quality of his early style. Even when Clarke is hewing closely to the traditions of descriptive realism, his sentences contain a digressive energy, an elliptical quality that allows them to blur time and space. Clauses beget clauses, subjects and objects pile up, perspective is lost and regained, and as the sentences unspool across the page, they thicken reality. The effect is sometimes frustrating, sometimes utterly disarming: after pages of frenetic stream of consciousness, the prose will snap suddenly into place. In many cases, meaning doesn't so much emerge as emanate, to the extent that it would be difficult to say what, exactly, a Clarke story is about. If someone were to ask me what happens in, say, "Four Stations in His Circle," from Clarke's 1971 collection, the only answer I could responsibly give would be to read the story in its entirety. Every word and comma builds toward its total signification; the only way to understand Clarke's best prose is to experience it.

These questions are not simply aesthetic. In order to appreciate the extent to which Clarke's oeuvre represents a fifty-year engagement with questions of nationalism, diaspora, empire, Blackness, and belonging, one must understand the way Clarke's style imprints meaning on the raw material of his narratives. Clarke's style flies in the face of the critics and academics who have frequently sought to reduce him to the role of a glorified journalist, a chronicler of Black experience who wrote what he saw, as if he had never really stopped writing for the *Timmins Daily News*. But it is precisely the aspects of Clarke's writing that are most often passed off as difficult (the circularity, the digressiveness) that impart the most meaning. Nowhere is this more apparent than in his late-career novels *The Polished Hoe* and *More*, and his astonishing final memoir *'Membering*.

Clarke's final books masterfully revisit the great obsessions that animated his early and mid-career work. *The Polished Hoe*, set in 1950s Barbados, follows the protagonist Mary-Mathilda over the course of a single night as she slowly, and in circular fashion, gives a deposition to Sargeant Percy Stuart explaining why she killed her father and former lover, Mr. Bellfeels. *More* follows Idora Morrison over the course of four purgatorial days while she waits for her son BJ to return home. *'Membering* builds out from Clarke's first memoir, *Growing Up Stupid Under the Union Jack*, to cover his school days in Barbados, his years of struggle in Toronto, his sojourns in America and Barbados, his adventures in politics, and his meditations on race, slavery, colonialism, and Canadian culture. Different in content, the books are united by a sensuality of language, a denseness of allusion, a keenness of insight, and a baroque, circular style of narration that, formally, lies between the improvisational flair of bebop and the mathematical discipline of the fugue.

Consider this long passage from one of *'Membering*'s most remarkable chapters, "The Green Door House," which sees Clarke's fascination with a particular Toronto house morph and intensify as he travels to Cuba, Venice, France, and Holland:

> It takes me five minutes to walk from my house to the St. Lawrence Hall, which I have to pass to get to the St. Lawrence Market, which is my destination. Years ago, before 1873, when the house was built and after 1492, my future and my present disposition were discussed and quarrelled about in this St. Lawrence Hall. I walk past the St. Lawrence Hall now, to buy pigs' feet, ham hocks, plantains, okras, and pigtails in the market itself. And nowadays, I go to the St. Lawrence Hall to receive the Trillium Prize for Literature, and to drink wine and eat thick slices of cheese at other functions—weddings, book launches, and dances. When I pass the post office, midway to the hall, reputedly the first

post office in Toronto, and I pick up snippets of history from the neighbourhood newspaper, I add to the "facts" of that history, the real truth, the "narrative" coached by the spirits and the myths, and I conclude that the man who lived in this green-door house, in 1876, three years after it was built, was a slave—whether in chains still, or "freed," or manumitted, or spared the hangman's knot thrown round a branch of a magnolia tree—if there are no magnolia trees in Canada, then I still say magnolia tree, to denote the symbolism, for it doesn't matter. (261)

Clarke entwines memory and imagination, history and myth to create a dense network of signification. A short walk to the market brings to mind the history of abolition in Toronto, Columbus's fateful arrival in the Caribbean, Clarke's own literary celebrity, the West Indian food that signifies his immigrant origins and also, for readers familiar with Toronto's St. Lawrence Market, suggests a particular kind of arrival of West Indian culture in Canada in general. In many ways a fine example of Clarke's mastery of stream-of-consciousness narration, the apparently random nature of the musings is belied by the insistent return to the dissonant, omnipresent theme of slavery and colonization. The appearance of chaos masks an underlying focus and obsessiveness, one that imparts to the reader a sense both of limitless consciousness and profound historical claustrophobia.

In Clarke's late style, repetitive digression is turned to philosophical ends. Characters circle back to the same words, phrases, stories, and ideas, and the plot is constantly doubling back on itself before moving forward before doubling back again. It is often hard to tell when a scene is taking place, or who is speaking, or whether what they are describing is real or imagined. In the virtuosic sentence that opens *More*, Idora Morrison, lying in bed in her basement apartment, hears the bells of the cathedral, mentally traverses the streets of Toronto, remembers arriving in Canada as a domestic worker, and starts worrying about her son BJ, and *that man*, his father. In *The Polished Hoe*, Mary-Mathilda's deposition becomes the story of her entire life, the story of her mother's life, the story of the island of Barbados, and eventually, in a way, the story of the entire Caribbean. The chronotope embodied in Clarke's style is one in which the Middle Passage and the trauma of slavery are consistently made present through the characters' imaginations and memories, and through the material conditions of the world around them.

For Clarke, the light playing across a green door late one afternoon is remembered in the sunlight along Havana's Malecón, and the doors of houses in Bordeaux built from money made on the slave trade. But the connections made in the minds of Clarke and his characters are not, in fact, random: they arise from the historical truth that few places on earth were left materially unaffected by slavery and the Triangle Trade. Toronto and Bridgetown are bound together by history, as both cities are connected through London, Paris, New York, and the slave castles of the Gold Coast. The shared history of colonialism has created deep connections between disparate cultures, and the profound inequality and violence intrinsic to the structures of colonialism is manifested in ways both material and immaterial. Clarke's style reflects the way Black diasporic people's relationship to familial, national, and institutional structures in the West is haunted by their brutal experiences of empire—what Christina Sharpe has called "monstrous intimacies." By returning again and again to these deep and long-standing spatial relationships, Clarke's style both affirms his characters right to exist and build lives in Toronto while also subverting the paternalistic liberal notion that by "welcoming" West Indians Canada is playing the role of the generous multicultural state. If peoples from every corner of the earth can be found in Toronto, perhaps that is because no part of the world has been free from the destructive meddling of the British Empire.

One of Clarke's more brilliant and enigmatic flourishes in *More* is to have Idora repeatedly claim that she was born in Canada when asked about her origins. Elsewhere, of course, she proudly declares herself to be "pure Barbadian," and we know from other passages in the novel that she came to Canada as a young woman (118). On the level of narrative, Idora seems to be challenging the common racist assumption that a Black person could not actually be "from" Canada; but she is also, perhaps, making a more significant political claim: being born "here" and being from Barbados are not mutually exclusive. After all, to invert an old CanLit cliché, here is where? Idora is, in one sense, an immigrant, but she is also "from" the same place Canada is from: the British Empire. This is underlined playfully in a passage from *The Polished Hoe*: Mary-Mathilda and Sargeant Percy Stuart are having a conversation about English goods and brands, and when Mary-Mathilda tells Sargeant that Red Rose Tea isn't English, but Canadian, he responds with sardonic confidence that Canada is "Still the British Empire!"

A Cosmopolitanism of the Colonized

Ignored for much of his career, Clarke is in the process of being vindicated by a new generation—one he had helped mentor and raise up—who are using his writing as a jumping-off point for their own novels about Black Canadian experiences and their own blistering indictments of anti-Blackness in Canada. This is due to the fact that, in many ways, CanLit has changed significantly since the 1960s: writers like Esi Edugyan, Rawi Hage, Madeleine Thien, Dionne Brand, David Chariandy, Rohinton Mistry, and André Alexis receive national recognition for their work, and Canadian publishers are publishing more work by writers of colour.

But some things are still depressingly similar. Anti-Blackness remains a salient issue in publishing, and for every writer of colour who wins the Giller, there are dozens who labour in obscurity. Given all this, the desire to anoint Clarke a full-blooded Canadian deserving of a place in the pantheon alongside Atwood and Birney and Richler is more than understandable. Clarke left a deep and lasting mark on this country's literary scene, and it would be impossible to understand the evolution of Canadian letters without taking account of his presence. Who could possibly argue that his career doesn't mark a central achievement of Canadian literature?

I confess, however, that the impulse to wrap Clarke in the flag and fold his legacy into the story of CanLit leaves me a little uneasy. Protectionism and parochialism were the most lasting legacy of Canadian literary publishing in the 1960s and '70s, and being a Canadian all too frequently seems to foreclose the possibility of being anything else. Clarke understood perhaps better than any other Canadian writer of his generation that the nationalism espoused by Commonwealth countries in the post-colonial period was shallow soil for a serious writer, and the depth of his writing is a feature of his cosmopolitanism, both as a man and as a thinker. Perhaps his most enduring contribution to world literature is his exploration of what cosmopolitanism means for the colonized, whose ancestors were stolen from Africa and who were in turn forced to migrate to the North because of economic pressures brought on by the no less perfidious machinery of globalization.

This cosmopolitanism is neither rootless nor utopian; it is not programmatic, and it does not deal in solutions. Instead, it is a process of uncovering, through hard experience, the profound connections that exist between disparate places and peoples, a critical awareness that the world we live in is the product of history, and that understanding that history, meditating on it, making it present in our lives, is necessary if we are to live honestly. Clarke's characters are often deluded (usually by themselves), and when their stories end tragically it is usually because of their inability or refusal to see what was in front of their eyes. If his books contain a moral, it is that the only way to see through the structures and ideologies that rule over us is by paying close attention to the world around us, to the architecture of our cities, the food on our plates, the language in our mouths, the cut of our clothes, and the thoughts in our heads. If his work offers hope, it is the difficult hope of great literature: that being less deceived about the powers that animate the world and distort our lives may not make us happier or better, but it will make us wiser, and wisdom is its own reward.

For those who write in Canada today, perhaps the most precious lesson Clarke offers is that we can be at home in Canada without believing in Canada, that the moral fate of this country is irreducibly bound to the fate of the modern world, that political acuity and ethical judgment do not need to come at the cost of style, beauty, and grace. Clarke has earned his place as a foundational figure in the literary history of this country. But I believe it would be a shame if this man, this raconteur, this lexical demolition artist who contained and gave birth to so many worlds were to have his significance finally reduced to having been, for better or for worse, the angriest Black man in Canada.

Note

1   Clarke earned this sobriquet after *Maclean's* published "A Black Man Talks about Race Prejudice in White Canada," one of several high-profile essays he wrote about Canadian racism in the mid-1960s.

CHAPTER 23

I Can Say I Read It

E. Martin Nolan

After Austin Clarke's "When He Was Free and Young and He Used to Wear Silks" and "Sometimes a Motherless Child"

I: Pilot Tavern, Toronto

This place does not rumble with your ghost,
Austin. That's the construction next door.
Just as you knew, this city's under the drill.
I'm in the building you were in but it's in
a different place now. No one wears silks.
Or maybe they do wear silks here. Under the drill
in Yorkville, in silks. The drilling in the wall keeps up,
and no one pays it mind. Because it's empty.
Because of the drilling. You sang in that long poem
that romance was fleeting. That you had it
in here, in a building that was in another place,
in this city that crushes steady and slow,
so gradual, the ease passes unnoticed,
dust in overpriced coffee on a sidewalk patio
kicked up in the rush by the gigging so much
they pass with a sound like distant wind.

II: Artist's Residency, Finland

White boy, white country, another great white north.
I'm a few days at the retreat, looking out on pale yellow fields
of almost ripe rye, striped green over the gentle hills down
to a shallow lake dense with lilies. So far from Bathurst Street—
so far from your Bathurst, Austin, is our Bathurst. Toronto
tears it all down before it's old enough to keep around.

Like the falling forests of MacGregor Park, doomed in the rocky,
      shallow soil
against Lake Huron. MacGregor: a Scottish name. Clarke,
      Nolan: Irish.
That doesn't bind us more than an airport Irish pub
where only the rich or stupid can get drunk.

A Black man drove the cab we took after arriving off the ferry
      in Helsinki.
Two white families ahead of us passed him by and went
to the white drivers behind him. Austin, a good white man
in your story is the Finnish landlord. I've read that far, and
      I believe
in coincidences. Granite is everywhere here, like Ontario.

III: The Pages

Austin, I've been reading further. The PDF cuts off
the last pages. BJ and Marco are spectres
in the story's imagination, locked away from me,
floating, distant as the kindness of the landlord
from the back seat of the Toronto PD cruiser.

I go online, but cannot find it. No one here
is allowed online but me, as I leave early.

And so, I am the only one who knows
about the shootings in El Paso and Dayton.

No barrier can be put to human violence. Austin,
I'm full of it, and I spray it toward your ghost like soft bullets.

IV: The Pages

Bathurst, a British name. A Lord. Dundas, British. A Lord. Bloor,
    Eglinton, King, Queen,
British, British. The museum the cop drives BJ past: Royal.
    Spadina—
"slow rise" in Algonquin—Ontario, these English butcheries
of Native names the only respite from the never-ending British
of the names of Toronto, the routes of BJ's torture, his mother's
    torture.

V: Halifax

Still haven't finished the story. Still the cop rides those kids
    around, trying
to decipher the history of hate he holds in his unprepared soul.
    Hate loves

an unprepared soul. I've come to the new central library, and sit
    on a terrace
looking out onto the giant beautiful harbour. They don't have
    the book.

They have five of your other books. They have them in the
    "Black Fiction" section.
That's in the back of the fiction section, which is not called
    "White Fiction."

The terrace is full of kids. A laughing racial mix. One little girl
    turns to another,
sitting alone, just off to the side. The first girl pauses, and
    freestyles a song. Goes:

"you're a small child sitting on a table," even though the other
    girl sits on a chair,
clearly. They laugh, because this is a funny way to be wrong. A
    good way.

CHAPTER 24

Austin Clarke's Books

Katherine McKittrick

> To a book collector, you see, the true freedom of all
> books is somewhere on his shelves.
> —Walter Benjamin, "Unpacking My Library"

> Does the order of books determine the order of things?
> —Homi Bhabha, "Unpacking My Library Again"

Rinaldo Walcott introduced me to Austin Clarke during the early
stages of my PhD studies at York University. I hoped that visiting
Austin Clarke would help me think about Black geographies. At
that time, I was imagining the tensions between Black diasporic
geographies (globally scattered populations not necessarily visible
through diagrammatic representation; the Black Atlantic) and
colonial or Eurocentric geographies (diagrammatic representation; positivist cartographies). Working in the fields of human
geography and Black studies, I explored how traditional mapping
practices, such as documenting where Black people *are*, often
erased, misrepresented, or watered down the complex spaces
and places inhabited by Black diasporic communities; I looked to
the work of Black intellectuals and cultural producers who drew
attention to how they challenged these misrepresentations. Early
in the research program, I ambitiously wanted to "map" the Black

Diaspora. I wanted to provide a kind of diagrammatic representation without the mandate for conquest. This, I soon learned, was not a helpful orienting frame for my project—although it was a frame that required an attempt and failure. While visiting Austin Clarke I fell in love with his bookshelves. I took photographs of the bookshelves. The bookshelves consisted of built-ins, smaller cabinets, some with glass, bookracks; coffee tables and the floor also served as book storage. The books on the built-ins were mostly hardcover, mostly first editions. There were hundreds of them. Some of Austin Clarke's own first-edition texts were in one of the smaller bookracks—*The Prime Minister, Proud Empires*. There were doubles: two copies of *Cambridge* by Caryl Phillips, for example. There were photographs within the shelves as well as paintings and sketches and drawings. Photographs of family and friends. His daughter's university degree hung beside the built-ins on the east side. Norman Mailer, Djanet Sears, Michael Ondaatje, a sign reading "Austin's Archives." LeRoi Jones. *The History of East Africa. Voices of a Black Nation.* The collected book series on Bernard Montgomery. *White Over Black: American Attitudes Toward the Negro, 1550–1812* by Winthrop Jordan. *Eight Men.* Zora Neale Hurston. Pushkin. C.L.R. James, *Cricket. Tutu* by Miles Davis . . . just one visible vinyl record cover, facing forward: *Tutu.*

I asked Austin Clarke how he organized his bookshelves. He told me he tried to organize the books by genre and according to the geographic location of the author. So poetry from the United States would go here, and British histories would go there, and novels from Canada would be beside that. A biography of Margaret Laurence is one shelf above the biographies of Brian Mulroney, Paul Martin. Poetry from Canada might be, though, way over there, on the other side of the room.

Following Austin Clarke's coordinates—genre and geography—I studied the shelves. There were patterns: V.S. Naipaul was shelved and collected alongside other texts that held the coordinates: Trinidad, novel. Winston Churchill too; his coordinates were: England, biography. T.S. Eliot was in multiple places:

US, UK, poetry, biography, plays/drama. T.S. Eliot moves. Richard Wright moves too. I saw (what I thought were) inconsistencies: *Fidel and Religion* beside *Pushkin* beside *Altogether Elsewhere: Writers on Exile* beside *Juneteenth.* The coordinates—genre and geography—were imperfect. Then: the spines of Wilson Harris. The ornate dust jackets. *The Four Banks of the River of Space.*

In his essay on book collecting, "Unpacking My Library," Walter Benjamin tells us that books invite a mood, "not an elegiac mood but, rather, one of anticipation" (59). A few paragraphs later Benjamin writes that we have a relationship to books, books as objects, "which does not emphasize their functional, utilitarian value—that is their usefulness—but studies and loves them as the scene, the stage, of their fate" (60). If we think Benjamin's insights on books (as objects of unhinged anticipation and love scene) alongside Austin Clarke's coordinates (genre and geography),

Austin Clarke's bookshelves.
Permissions: William Ready Division of Archives and Research Collections, McMaster University Library

modernity unfurls. *Flâneur. Plantation. Auction.* Baruch Spinoza. North Africa. Vladimir Lenin. Jamaica. Poet. Cuba. Novel. Plot. Read. Read for more than words.

In *Playing in the Dark*, Toni Morrison teaches us to notice that our narrative worlds are "wholly racialized" (5). She teaches us that plot-making is tied to meditations on a freedom that is enacted as racial terror. She shows us how to read and come to know the novel outside of itself. Toni Morrison allows us to think about how the novel rests on other (Black) worlds without necessarily naming or humanizing those worlds. Her instruction asks us, I think, to see and read Austin Clarke's bookshelves outside of themselves. The coordinates, because they are imperfect, open up a way to also read vertically down, instead of across and in frame. Diagonal. Naipaul's island is undone, Churchill's too. Glass encasings are no longer suffocating. Visiting Austin Clarke, I learned that bookshelves are coordinates for what we cannot see but need to notice. I learned to read for unruly diasporic collaborations rather than comfortable diagrammatic patterns. I learned that books, as Dionne Brand put it in *A Map to the Door of No Return*, "leave much more than words." I learned that our books, and book collections, are sites of ambivalence, and that the books—the spines, the dust jackets, the pages, the volumes shelved imperfectly—are beautiful texts of anticipation. Genre and geography, buckling.

CHAPTER 25

Hyphen (for Austin "Tom" Clarke, 1934–2016)

John R. Lee

> To me, it's really so simple: life should be lived on the edge. You
> have to exercise rebellion, to refuse to tape yourself to the rules,
> to refuse your own success, to refuse to repeat yourself, to see
> every day, every year, every idea as a true challenge. Then you
> will live your life on the tightrope.
>
> —Philippe Petit

I. high wire

> the figure in black called his dangerous act a "coup"
> the press: "outrageous," "audacious," "artistic crime
> of the century"—
> I imagine the abyss of New York below his tight-rope

crazy man. The photos disturb
my gut. Angels had to have held him up.
And suppose he had fallen like a demon to the curbs
of Lower Manhattan? Too high for me that science, stupefying
such aerial defiance at the inch-wide edge of the brink—
on the thin wing of his pole, sauntering that stratosphere

indestructible, who scripted 9/11 and all that broke
and fell into itself that day, those girders, those heights,
the falling man, the conflagrated wires, the vaporized ropes?

II. hyphen

the Black, dreadlocked figure of Tom Clarke
crosses the cold, clear span of the hyphen
of Canadian space, striking

out over the white vast of its lakes, plains
diasporic cities and other chasms,
stepping between ziggurats of Babylon

their steel and glass tablets of encrypted racism
negotiating the insistent subtraction of face from nation—
on the fiction of his pole, his arrogance striding those
high places

he defies thin thresholds of fear, for Albert Johnson
Emmet Till, Soweto, the charred churches
for Malcolm, Nina Simone, his chattel-house Bajans.

CHAPTER 26

"Myth Grounded in Truth": Sound, Light, and the Vertical Imagination in Austin Clarke's *'Membering*

Winfried Siemerling

When Austin Clarke's memoir *'Membering* appeared in 2015, I had occasion again to reflect on a writer whose work I had come back to time and again over the years. It was instructive to follow Clarke's early wrestling with Toronto life, to read the entertaining accounts of his Harlem adventures looking for Baldwin but finding—and interviewing—Malcolm X, and of his involvements in politics; and it was enlightening to read the analyses of his own early novels, including his observations on the (lack of) models in that period, on the meaning of literary ancestors, and on CanLit and the Toronto literary scene at the time.

Among these autobiographical and literary riches, however, it was a short chapter that arrived a little after the halfway mark of the text that attracted my particular attention. Entitled "The Green Door House," it begins with a reflection—seemingly unconnected or even out of place at first as one peruses the following paragraphs—about the singular power of music to conjure, without warning and with great force, a vast number of memories and emotions that come to the listener with sudden immediacy.

Writes Clarke: "I find myself sometimes, at odd moments, with no preparation for my recollection of song, nor any indication that the words of the verses have still remained in my memory; but when these snatches of memories come to me, like a spasm of history, I recall most of the lyrics, and certainly that part which must have struck me as relevant, or personally touching, when first the 'membering of the tune struck me" (251).

The power of the aural also shines forth in an earlier comment by Clarke in the volume; memorizing jazz pieces like Miles Davis's "Flamenco Sketches" and Coltrane solos in their entirety lightened his winter walks in the absence of an unaffordable Walkman. Now, however, he cites the uncontrollable, overpowering, and irruptive force of Whitney Houston's "I Wanna Dance with Somebody." Suddenly, "like a spasm of history," other past instances flood Clarke's memory, and moments where her artistry, like that of Ray Charles on another remembered occasion, seemed to vanquish racial animosity, and signalled to him that "once more a black American was showing the light to the vast, overwhelming white America" (252).

After this opening, the narrative shifts to another register, and only later in the chapter and the volume will the connection with the opening reveal itself obliquely—although a sense of the compositional intricacies and frequent tonal recodings of jazz transitions lingers. The shift is heralded by the chapter title's reference to the colour green. Clarke now recounts his attraction to a house "conspicuous for its green-painted door, cut vertical into two halves, so that only half opened to let you enter; and this house has stood out in my attention because of the way the lights settle on it, in a soft sensual sensation." "This house," Clarke continues, "pulled me toward it, in a trance-like communication, to face the spirits and the myths of my history" (252). We could note that the door, cut vertically in half, also limits entrance, blocking as much space as it opens, hiding as much as it reveals, while nonetheless letting you enter. But it is the light that works its strong visual effects on Clarke's 'membering and imaginative capability. It does so especially as the sun strikes the house "at the four o'clock angle of romance and seduction" that foreshadows communion with "the spirits and the myths of my history" (253). Some of the associations evoked by that phrase become clearer as the text progresses, but the modular force of light here lets his mind range widely—like a solo by Trane—over a number of locations and recognizable themes, only to come "home," as we will see, in several surprising turns. The evocative force of light takes Clarke to the primordial role it has in Italian painting; and hence to its revelation, on a palazzo wall in Vicenza, of a Roman numeral that in his mind translates into 1492—"the year Christopher Columbus 'discovered' me in Barbados, and others like me, in the Caribbean."

Columbus, we know, did not call on the author in Barbados, while historians will be quick to point out that he did not "discover" Barbados either (that was instead Pedro a Campos in 1536). The nature of Clarke's first statement will perhaps guide us, however, to also not read the second one literally—and in addition, to look in a similar way at the somewhat improvised transposition from Roman to Arabic numerals "according to my memory." I will return to this rather important point, but for now suffice it to say that the modular transition to 1492 and Columbus, together with the connecting motive of the blue waves of the sea, allow Clarke to initiate a chain of associations leading his memories through earlier travels, to Havana, Venice, Paris, and finally Bordeaux. The sequence traverses a Black Atlantic-cum-Mediterranean geography, guided by a theme that offers an extended meditation on the link between wealth and the slave trade.

Havana's Malecón, facing "the same water that Christopher Columbus travelled," with its dilapidated grandeur reminds Clarke of the city's former splendour; but it also leads his him to wonder about "the profits made from the Atlantic trade that came across Atlantic Ocean." During a subsequent trip to Venice, Clarke marvels about its water-based architecture and magnificence, yet he feels again impelled to ask: "where did all this Venetian wealth come from?" His answer includes not only trickery and trade but, more specifically, the slave trade. Although Venice had other sources of income, it is indeed true that it was active in the Mediterranean slave trade; in an all-important turn, however, Clarke will add: "But this is speculation. I do not have papyrus and old tomes to check against my fancy, and my fantasy. My narrative is built upon the strong foundation of myth. But there is the same pull, the same importance of light, the same hidden spirits in the buildings that surround me, in Toronto; and on the Malecón, and here in Venice. Who has the ownership of this history?"

During a subsequent visit to Bordeaux Clarke notes that the light on the city's water-facing buildings reminds him of the Malecón; his host surprises him by responding voluntarily: "These buildings you're seeing, all along this way, are the profits from the slave trade." Although speaking "without prompting," the French host seems to have caught the gist of Clarke's earlier musings about light: "It makes me feel I've been here, before. And I know I have not been here before. In a different sense. But I also know I have been here, before."

"In a Different Sense"

"In a different sense": one facet of this amplification appears as Clarke remembers a trip to Amsterdam, where he tours the canals. Again it is the light on the canal houses that reminds Clarke of Havana, Venice, Bordeaux, and also of the wharf in Barbados's Bridgetown: "All this history and history of architecture here in the Netherlands is bound up in slavery. 'Bound up' is the ironical intransitive verb. My history touches all of them: buildings in which I was tied up and flogged, but in which my spirits lived on." Clarke's use of the pronoun "I" tells us that, before physically arriving in Bordeaux, for instance, he had been there indeed, in a metonymic sense that also nourishes Langston Hughes's speaker in "The Negro Speaks of Rivers"—an all-encompassing "I" that has witnessed waterways and civilizations from a Black perspective, and that has retained, accumulated, and remembered the significance of that presence and experience.

But there is a further facet of this "different sense" evoked by Clarke, a sense that comes to the fore in connection with the green-door house. Clarke has mentioned the house also in the context of the other cities, adding at some point that he finally bought it and added a green awning over the green door. We learn that he is "thinking that this house, the one with the green door, built in 1863, could have been the residence of a man who fled to Canada, on the Underground Railroad, and who became 'a shoemaker.' And I turn the pages of history and of speculation faster," Clarke adds, "in order to get to the narrative of myth grounded in truth. And to see whose truth I am using; and whose truth it is." What Clarke is telling us is that the "narrative of myth," which in his memory leads across so many water-connected locations like a jazz musician's solo across key and chord changes, is "grounded" in a certain kind of positional truth that is not limited by facts. As he explains, "I add to the 'facts' of that history, the real truth, the 'narrative' coached but the spirits and the myths, and I conclude that the man who lived in this green-door house, in 1876, three years after it was built, was a slave." Clarke tells us that he bought the house after having passed it for fourteen years, and wonders whether the slave who became a shoemaker could "deliberately, and from the grave, have sent those spirits to alert me, and have me join them?"

There is a sense of a homecoming, here, as the chapter modulates back to its opening motives of voice-and-light-induced memory and of the green-door house's ability to pull the author, "in a trance-like communication, to face the spirits and the myths of my history." The force field of that "trance-like communication" has indeed determined the composition of the chapter, with its modal transitions ranging in transformative ways, and "in a different sense," across the reigns of factuality and truth. Clarke in his own distinctive style does here what other writers have done in their own ways to get to the bottom of things, and with the help of an imagination "grounded in truth" extract and create meaning from the multiform surfaces and appearances of reality. Clarke's reference to light, romance, and seduction, for instance, evoke the seductive effects that Hawthorne, in the "The Custom House," ascribed to the moonlight, a medium that for him "spiritualized" the daily objects around him and was "the most suitable for a romance-writer to get acquainted with his illusive guests" (and ghosts), creating a space "where the Actual and Imaginary may meet, and each imbue itself with the nature of the other" (*Scarlet Letter* 35, 46). The text Hawthorne thus introduced, *The Scarlet Letter*, also explored deeper historical truths with the help of a wide-ranging imagination.

Clarke's distinction between "facts" and "the real truth" also evokes, however, Toni Morrison's reflections on this matter; as she writes in "The Site of Memory," "the crucial distinction for me is not the difference between fact and fiction, but the distinction between fact and truth. Because facts can exist without human intelligence, but truth cannot" (72). And if we want to home in further on Clarke's specific handling of the communicative traffic between meaning and the past, his ending reminds us of the more possessive force of the particular spirits that are active in his chapter and that continue to "ride" him, as he says: those spirits call him to his green-door house, a home whose vertically divided door also opens on the Black Atlantic and its history. These possessive spirits are of Caribbean ancestry, as becomes clear when Clarke refers here to his mother's knowledge about "slavery and skeletons and witchcraft"; accepting this knowledge, Clarke concludes his chapter with the assertion that the "shoemaker's spirits ride me across the Atlantic Ocean, to the Malecón, to Venice, to Bordeaux, and now to Amsterdam."

Home

Yet it is not only that the improvisational journey of Clarke's chapter "homes" back to the opening motives of the evocative force of light and the pervasive yet often surprising presence of memory;

the chapter also speaks about a house that Clarke made his home. At a first glance, the "vertical" dimension of this home reveals an "unhomely" and gruesome reality: "So, each time I enter the right-hand half of the green door of the house, built in 1863, I think of all those other houses in Cuba in the Caribbean, in Bordeaux in France, in Venice in Italy, and in Amsterdam in the Netherlands, erected from the help of my sweat and floggings, from the bones in the basements with skeletons." The house thus succeeds indeed in making him face "the spirits and the myths of my history"; but this space also turns out to be home.

Here Clarke surprises us with another turn in his associative journey, a further modulation that makes space, in his "myth grounded in truth," for both the historical consequences of slavery and a notion of home. While referring at length to the brutality of French slavery in Haiti, Clarke can nonetheless write: "I am home in Paris." The city for him "reflects a relationship, that, in spite of its viciousness and its inequalities . . . involved me, in presence, in colour, in voice, and ironically, in labour and the profits made from my labour." As a consequence, Clarke comes to "think of the most foreign and unusual cities, as home. Havana. Toronto. Venice. Manchester. Bordeaux. Toulouse. Amsterdam. Paris." With this distinctive turn, Clarke takes personal possession of the "myths of my history." He lays claim to the wealth and splendour created by the enslaved, in a perspective that transforms victimization into rightful ownership. In a subsequent chapter that returns to some of these motives, "The Culture of Chains," Clarke makes this recoding of memory—a constant presence evoked by sound, light, and a "vertical" imagination—even more explicit. Recalling his visit to Amsterdam a second time, he remembers travelling its canals "in such a way that I feel I am going through the intestines of a city that fed upon the land and upon the people that came from islands in my part of the world; and in this shocking realization, I am not angry, I am not ashamed, I am not feeling as if I am a victim. I feel I am a partner. A senior partner. It was my 'wealth' of skin and sweat and culture that made the 'wealth' of Amsterdam and the Netherlands."

Clarke's recoding of the associations of victimization into a perspective that includes not just proprietorship, but indeed *senior* partner status with its concomitant claims to control, reveals a way of living "in the wake" that also articulates insistent forms of belonging; it is a narrative "built upon the strong foundation of myth" that claims ownership of history as a form of home (but may also yet continue to be present in claims for material reparations). Hortense Spillers is among those who have tried to spell out the stakes and challenges in changing the kinds of myth that Clarke's 'membering is working to transform. Certain designations, Spillers writes in *Black, White, and in Color: Essays on American Literature and Culture,* "are markers so loaded with mythical prepossession that there is no easy way for the agents buried beneath them to come clean. . . . In order for me to speak a truer word concerning myself, I must strip down through layers of attenuated meanings, made an excess in time; over time, assigned by a particular historical order, and there await whatever marvels of my own inventiveness" (65).

Clarke's celebratory meditation and memory-driven improvisation on the motive of the green-door house put the "marvels" of his "own inventiveness" to incisive use. In the process of 'membering, we see Clarke make himself a(t) home in Toronto and its history while connecting his experiences to a transnational sense of belonging that manages to distill resilience and pride from a history of dispersal and devastation. Having taken possession of his abode, and responding in "trance-like communication" to the spirits of history in acts of 'membering that bring forth transformative "myth grounded in truth," Clarke in the end "knew that I was wise in purchasing the green-house door."

CHAPTER 27

À St. Matthias

George Elliott Clarke

For Oni Joseph

Robert Sandiford snaps my colourized photo
at grey-stone St. Matthias Anglican Church

just outside sea-bleached Bridgetown, Barbados.
Whimsically, we stopped here because Austin C.

Clarke was a boy here. The sun's now as white
as the stones where Bro' Austin worshipped

an Anglo-Saxon Christ, his stiff upper lip never
trembling when the whips and spears struck.

And there's the sapphire sea, a lowered sky,
blue jewellery, sparking mid dark-green trees,

and the sea churns white among the grey stones,
and the Parliament is a whited sepulchre

at the slave auction site where it now sits,
while the Atlantic crows at blanching sand,

And then Robert's auto dies, forcing us to walk,
cursing, blaspheming, in Austin's footsteps.

CHAPTER 28

Clarke on Clarke

George Elliott Clarke
& Paul Barrett

George Elliott Clarke's poetry and criticism includes a sustained engagement with the work, influence, and style of Austin Clarke. His two major collections of essays, Odysseys Home: Mapping African-Canadian Literature *(2002) and* Directions Home: Approaches to African-Canadian Literature *(2011), include a number of essays dedicated to Austin Clarke's work. More recently, he has offered poetic reinterpretations of Clarke's "When He Was Free and Young and He Used to Wear Silks" in his collection of poems,* Gold, *and in* Matrix Magazine.*

Paul Barrett interviewed George Elliott Clarke in April 2017 to understand these poetic reinterpretations, his take on Austin Clarke's importance to Canadian literature, and his contribution to Black writing in Canada and internationally.

Paul Barrett: I'd like to start by thinking a bit about some of your recent homages or transformations of Austin's work, particularly "When He Was Free and Young and He Used to Wear Silks." I'm thinking of the pieces in *Gold* and *Matrix*, where you have these two reinterpretations. What led you to return to these early parts of Austin's work?

George Elliott Clarke: I became acquainted with Austin's work through the short stories and essays, primarily from the 1980s and into the 1990s. I had an opportunity to do an anthology of African-Canadian literature, or Black Canadian writing if one prefers, for McClelland and Stewart [*Eyeing the North Star: Directions in African-Canadian Literature*], and I knew right away that "Free and Young" was the story I was going to reprint in that anthology.

I remember it also because of the fact that Austin was represented by Denise Bukowski, who is also my agent. In fact, she became my agent because of her unwavering determination that Austin was going to receive five hundred dollars for that story!

Anyway, I had to have that story. Of course, it's indebted to Joyce and his stream-of-consciousness technique. However, I love the fact that that story—keeping in mind that it is difficult to follow completely the speaker's thoughts—is a great take on early 1970s Toronto, the era of the Black Arts movement, the cultural politics of the time, the rise of second-wave feminism and how it began to impact relationships in terms of divorce becoming more common, and the praxis of the "hookup" becoming more widespread. Here's this protagonist who is thinking about various relationships—in the midst of probably attempting to seduce someone else, who reminds him of this other woman that he knew. There are numerous layers in the story as well as a great mix of contradictory attitudes as well as references to 1970s pop culture and politics. Here's an African- or Caribbean-Canadian riffing off of life in progressive, hippy Toronto and the arrival of soul culture along with the increasing presence of Caribbean-Canadians and the real-life impact of the politics of feminism. There is nothing else like it in Clarke's oeuvre or in Anglo-Canadian literature.

P.B.: It's interesting, given the complicated style of this story and just how modernist or even avant-garde it is, that it is so rarely taken up by Canadian critics. This is particularly puzzling given the tendency of Canadian critics to engage in sociological readings of Clarke's work: to miss the form and treat his work as mere "reporting" of Black life in Canada. Here is a story in which the form of the work screams out for attention yet doesn't receive it.

G.E.C.: A couple of CanLit academics that I spoke to—about fifteen years ago—about "When He Was Free and Young" critiqued the story as being antisemitic and implied that it could not be canonical for this reason. Of course, I recognize that there are phrases and sentences in the story where the speaker offers his critique of what *he perceives* as a Jewish tendency to avoid outright confrontation around civil rights agitation and to allow Black people—African-Americans specifically—to bear the brunt of the blowback, so to speak, or repression of the state, while themselves benefitting from the liberations effected by Black agitation. These are unfortunate comments, to put it mildly, but they are true to the psyche of the protagonist. In my take on "When He Was Free," I omit all those ethnocentric comments on the part of the protagonist. But I do read the original story in the context of the Black Power politics of the times, which had a hard edge, which was critical of what some radicals thought to be the collusion of some elements of Jewish-American society to support, if not the state, then at least state repression of African-Americans as a means of deflecting the state's antisemitic impulses. This critique goes back to Malcolm X, but was taken up by Amiri Baraka most stridently.

These are extremely unfair attitudes that Austin Clarke's protagonist does repeat, somewhat. Again, my impression of these elements is that they are a relatively minor aspect of the story, which does not mean that that they can be excused or ignored. However, the story's major thrust has to do with this particular middle-aged, middle-class, *Playboy*-ogling protagonist trying to get his romantic life, his sex life, "together"—to use appropriate, sixties slang—while the society, especially in terms of heterosexual relations, is changing rapidly. Changing under his feet, so to speak, while he's sitting at the Pilot Tavern.

Nevertheless, there's an absolutely objectionable antisemitic taint in Clarke's oeuvre that I've discussed critically. I'm very much aware, for instance, of a pamphlet, published back in 1967, that Clarke issued under a pseudonym, that does express, bluntly and blatantly, antisemitic commentary. "Black Man in a White Land" is the title, wherein Clarke—as Ali Kamal Al Kadir Sudan—is interviewed pseudonymously by Marvin X, an African-American writer who lived briefly in Canada in the late 1960s, early 1970s.

P.B.: Yes, and I think there are passages in his other work—*The Meeting Point*, for instance—that I think can be described as decidedly antisemitic. Particularly the depiction of Mr. Burrmann.

G.E.C.: Yes, so in confronting those passages, it's *possible* to perceive how some folks may have decided that it was okay to essentially give Mr. Clarke his due—as a Black writer on Black issues—but otherwise ignore work that can be problematic—not just antisemitic, but also homophobic and sexist, at times. Which is to say, his work reflects who he was. This does not excuse any of his objectionable utterances. However, just as we are able to make intellectual judgments about and maintain a critique of other objectionable writers while also being able to appreciate what is powerful and striking and important in their work, so do I think that Austin Clarke is eligible for the same kind of engagement with his controversial passages. However, to return to "When He Was Free and Young," there's plenty to engage with productively in that story without needing to fixate on the minute gestures toward ethnocentrism on the part of the fictitious speaker. To look at it another way, the anonymous speaker's sexism, buffeted by second-wave feminism, is the real crux and dynamic of the story.

P.B.: Indeed, another dimension of Clarke's writing that critics often find troubling is his depiction of women. Was this a concern for you in your rewriting of "When He Was Free and Young"? To add to that, you've talked about Clarke's use of the Canada-as-white-whore metaphor in some of his other writing. Was that in your mind as you wrote these tributes?

G.E.C.: Not really, because I think "When He Was Free" is far more personal. Clarke's not thinking as *socially* as he is in some other stories, such as "When the Bough Breaks" or "Canadian Experience," where Canada-as-white-whore metaphors appear. See, particularly, the introduction to *Nine Men Who Laughed*, when Clarke refers to the system—or "shitstem"—as having an aspect of Black male bashing that could be related to white dread of Black masculinity *and* white female dread of Black masculinity. But I don't see these concerns as central to "When He Was Free and Young."

But to return to the central question of whether Clarke's characters says unsavoury things about women: Yes, absolutely, they do. But does this mean we shouldn't read Clarke? I have to say, no.

Certainly in my mind, I align Austin Clarke with Mordecai Richler, who was also known to make comments that people took umbrage with. He was nevertheless an extremely important writer in CanLit. I think Clarke deserves to be considered alongside him as someone who did not hesitate to offer an unsparing, although tinged with satire, view of what he saw as the *real* purpose of racism, in particular, but also classism and sexism.

I do think that, though he's a little bit confused and a little bit drunk, the protagonist in "When He Was Free and Young" would like to be successful with these women in the Pilot Tavern, but he's also grudgingly understanding that things are changing, whether he likes it or not. He has to find a way forward—to forge principled, loving relationships—but is unsure how, which actually was probably the situation for a lot of heterosexual men, of whatever ethnic, racial, or cultural background, at the time. I think Clarke is honest about his protagonist in thinking through all of these new dilemmas.

Philip Roth's *Portnoy's Complaint* is potentially another text to place alongside Clarke's story, at least in this regard. So I think, frankly, it's really unfair to castigate Clarke for his political incorrectness while giving many other writers completely free berth and free reign to be as free-spiritedly objectionable in a "truth-telling" or satirical manner as they wish to be.

P.B.: I wonder if this has to do with the complicated nature of his politics, particularly the difficulty of Clarke being inadequately radical for the campus radicals, being too outspoken for conservatives. He'll rail against Canadian structures of race and class, the vertical mosaic, but one senses he's mostly angry that he's not at the top. In other words, Clarke is never completely at home within any of our traditional political nomenclatures.

G.E.C.: Yes, that's a fair assessment. Yet, we have been inadequate ourselves in just understanding how radical Clarke's perspective is. I sometimes make the point that generally speaking—and, yes, I am generalizing a lot here—African-American writers and intellectuals almost consistently make this argument: "Why can't we be treated equally?" Of course it's a fair and appropriate argument to make in a republic based on the idea of general equality. In fact, when it's clear that folks are being treated unequally, it is a cry to arms, a call to arms, for all of those disaffected persons to demand their equality under the Constitution. So Austin practically stands alone—in terms of internationally acclaimed writers, African-heritage writers—when he implies, "I don't want to be equal; I deserve to be recognized as naturally superior" [*laughs*].

That, to me, is an extremely radical statement. That's the satire, for me, in his writing. Clarke positions his protagonists as having to live Canadian immigrant lives that are slightly, or completely, fraudulent, because they don't want to live lives as obviously underclass folks. They come from backgrounds where they had property, were treated with respect, and attended elite schools, so why should the "colour of their skin" or the fact that they are Black suddenly entail their tumbling into the basement of this hierarchical, class-oriented monarchy? Why can't they step out of an upper-middle-class existence in the Caribbean or in India or in other parts of the world, come to Canada, and become prime minister, be premier, be the heads of corporations, be the presidents of universities, be police chief, be fire chief, and all without question or without having to struggle?

His characters often already have the pedigree and the educational accoutrements, the degrees, to be at the top. So why do they have to take a subsidiary, tertiary position? Why do they have to scrap and struggle when, in some cases, they are the sons and daughters of Caribbean prime ministers and/or Third World cabinet ministers?

That's the problematic that Clarke engages so powerfully—and that might also be a reason why folks are so hesitant to take him up. Because if the answer to Clarke's implicit socio-political challenge is "you should be our superiors and, at the top, and we should be your servants," well, what happens if you take that argument seriously, keeping in mind its satirical side?

Yet, it's only by taking that argument seriously that we can truly achieve real equality. If our social equality can imagine and *tolerate*—to use a great Canadian verb—the idea that there's a Black prime minister, a brown prime minister, a yellow prime minister, a red prime minister—for crying out loud, if we can collectively tolerate this notion, then we get there faster, i.e., to a position of real equality.

P.B.: Do you think there is an argument to be made that Austin has always been out of step with CanLit? In the seventies, when Atwood is writing *Survival* and thematic criticism is emerging as a force, Austin's writing doesn't accord with that particular definition of CanLit. Then in the nineties, when CanLit is appearing increasingly transnational and global, and critics are questioning whether the nation still holds as a salient category of analysis— I'm thinking also about the debates between you and Rinaldo Walcott around space, and the place of Blackness in the nation—Austin returns to the nation or at least Canadian space as an important element of how one imagines Blackness here.

G.E.C.: To begin, we do have to set Austin in an international context—far more international than is the case for most Canadian writers in the 1960s and '70s. Some had great readerships in Canada, but not necessarily beyond these borders. Yet Austin did; he saw himself quite rightly as being in the same bailiwick as Sam Selvon, Andrew Salkey, Derek Walcott, Kamau Brathwaite et al. All of them were leaving the Caribbean, moving to other nations and writing in those nations as well as writing back to the homeland by introducing London, Toronto, Montreal, Paris, and New York to great Caribbean writing. So it's probable that he never thought of himself, early in his career, as a Canadian writer, but rather thought of himself as international, following in the footsteps of his expat African-American idols Richard Wright and James Baldwin.

I'll bring in another figure who thought of himself along the same lines: Irving Layton. A poet, Layton never identified much with Canadian nationalism or thematics. Sure, he wrote his wilderness and nature poems, but for the most part he saw himself as belonging to an international, Anglo-American group of writers, and he loved to base himself in Greece, Italy, or Spain, as opposed to writing about the Great White North from Cabbagetown in Toronto or La Main in Montreal.

Austin also saw himself as belonging to an international, Black cast of writers. C-A-S-T—although maybe we can add an "E" to the end of that word! So, Austin goes and interviews Malcolm X, follows Amiri Baraka in his political life, goes back to Barbados and tries to establish the Caribbean Broadcast Corporation. He also helps to start Black studies programs across the United States, even teaching up-and-coming Black critics—like Houston Baker.

The irony here, though, is that while Clarke was an international writer, he actually did give Canada tremendous forensic scrutiny, but not in a way that was flattering to Canadian sensibilities or the establishment. (In a strange sense, I can suddenly put Pierre Berton and Austin Clarke side by side: both being "natty" in their dress and public presences and erudition. But Berton was very much part of the establishment and Austin was not—or, well, not as much.)

So I have to come back to an element that some might take umbrage with, but it has to be said: there is something called "race"—and even though this is Canada, where "race" seems spectral, I must still wonder: if Austin were white, would he be experiencing the same kind of critical neglect? If he had decided not to focus on race and class as much as he does, would his career have suffered as much neglect as it has? Yes, many fine white writers may also complain about neglect. But Austin was quite a public presence and published in New York and London, and had an international reputation *before* many English-Canadian writers—before Alice Munro, Margaret Atwood, or Michael Ondaatje. So one cannot rule out racism or ethnocentrism as a cause for his ostracism.

P.B.: In addition to racism, I also wonder if this has to do with a kind of critical ineptitude where Canadian critics are simply ill-equipped to read Austin's writing. They don't read Selvon, they don't read Brathwaite, they don't understand Coltrane so they can't read his work in the contexts of the traditions upon which he is drawing. Furthermore, they don't see how he draws on and adapts Eliot, Joyce, O'Connor, and others in his work, so he is imagined as lacking a tradition.

G.E.C.: Absolutely. In a sense his work has been awaiting the arrival of scholars and critics who have some foundation in pan-African discourses around literature, politics, and society. Folks who've read a Frantz Fanon, Malcolm X and liked it! He's been awaiting the arrival of critics who are steeped in those influences that he had, which most white English-Canadian writers would not have had. (At least the francophone writers would have read Frantz Fanon! I'm sure that Pierre Trudeau read Fanon as closely as he read Mao!)

P.B.: At the same time, Austin must have been a figure of frustration for you because in many respects, as you've written, Clarke's work and his depiction of Blackness in Toronto becomes a metonym for Blackness in Canada and diasporic Blackness is a metonym for Africadian existence. So to what extent did you find yourself thinking, *Yes Austin deserves his due, but so do these other writers and others histories?*

G.E.C.: Like many other younger writers, I strongly admired Austin. At the same time his work was complicit with the generally lazy and maybe even racializing, or racist, Canadian viewpoint that the only real Black people in Canada were recent immigrants from the Caribbean. Or, the only *good* Black people in Canada were recent immigrants from a particular class of people from the Caribbean. My anecdote about this perception goes back twenty years, but I did describe, in *Odysseys Home*, my having overheard a white academic tell a West Indian–Canadian Black how much "better" she and others like her were in comparison to the historically present Black Canadians who are "passive" (i.e., "lazy").

This idea doesn't get voiced very much: that there is a pecking order among Blacks as far as white Canadians are concerned; that there are good Blacks and bad Blacks (i.e., indigent, illiterate, shiftless, prone to criminality). In truth, the historical Black community was marked by poverty, illiteracy, the experience of segregation, and legalized lynching, and general suppression. Although this community has been here for two hundred years, and established churches and so on, we have still been perceived as rogues, criminals, and layabouts who didn't contribute anything to Canada. Or we just don't exist; the destruction of Africville was a fleshing out of that belief that we should not exist anywhere within sight.

Because of the racist, sexist, and classist immigration system that Canada put in place they began to "welcome"—that isn't quite the right verb—African and Asian immigrants from the Caribbean, as of 1955, the incoming first generation tended to be students, if they were men. They were arriving, having already achieved, in many cases, really good educations in their homelands, and some were even already upper middle class. So even though they were subject to racism, they were also quite impressive to a lot of white Canadians, who would have realized that these Afro-Caribbean men in the 1950s and '60s—and I use this verb quite deliberately—"outclassed" them significantly.

So, white Canadians could then compare these incoming, well-educated, well-dressed, courteous, well-spoken new Black

Canadians with the "old line" who may have been, for generations, unskilled manual labourers, maids, domestics, and illiterate
and criminalized—thanks to the structural, political, economic
mechanisms that kept the historical Black community a despised
underclass almost up until the present. Ironically, however,
the racism that the historical Black community experienced
became—and has become—a problem for Caribbean-Canadians,
who now also face challenges in schooling, employment, and
criminal justice, the same systemic blights—plights—that the
historical African-Canadian community has faced, and struggled
against, for centuries.

The good news is, in the last fifteen to twenty years, there
has begun to be some kind of *rapprochement* or understanding
that the two communities—immigrant Blacks and "indigenous"
Blacks (Africadians)—actually do have the same struggles and
must show unity to respond to the white racism that we collectively experience.

To conclude: It is Austin Clarke's work, especially the later
work, that is the signal, the lighthouse directing all of us to begin
to understand that we do have common struggles across ethnici-
ties and across racial categories and across categories of "settled-
ness" or immigration that we must address if we are ever going to
achieve true equality.

CHAPTER 29

All He Wanted to Do Was Type

Michael A. Bucknor

The following was originally presented as a tribute at the Annual West Indian Literature Conference in Montego Bay, Jamaica, on October 5, 2016, by Dr. Michael A. Bucknor, associate professor in the Department of Literatures in English, Mona Campus, University of the West Indies.

On May 9, 2016, I visited Austin Clarke at St. Michael's Hospital in Toronto. Prior to my visit, I had serendipitously come into contact with Rinaldo Walcott, whom I had planned to email to find out how Austin was doing because the news trickling down to Jamaica through friends in Canada was that he was not doing well. Several months earlier (September 2015), I had gone to Canada to deliver a paper at McMaster University. The lecture was sponsored by the McMaster University Library and the Department of English and Cultural Studies, because the Austin Clarke archives had been the bedrock of that research project. Austin was delighted to be invited to the talk, and had indicated to me he was attending.

His short email of August 26, 2015 said: "Dear Michael, I hope to attend your lecture on September 15th. Good luck with your lecture! As man, Austin." In April of that year, I attended the Trinidad and Tobago Bocas Literary Festival in order to see Austin, who was scheduled to be present, but again ill-health prevented him from attending. So, through that contact with Rinaldo on April 27, 2016, while he was in the Bahamas, I learned Austin was in room 64 on the fourteenth floor of St. Mike's on Shuter and Victoria.

This trip to Canada was to visit the Austin Clarke archives, and I had scheduled lunch with poet Olive Senior and tea with my former student Ronald Cummings in Toronto that day. Olive, after lunch, kindly escorted me to St. Michael's, and I went up to the fourteenth floor and easily found Austin. His room had a few pictures and news reports on the walls identifying him as a significant Caribbean-Canadian writer. I went in the room and stood beside his bed. His eyes were bright, even as he laboured to breathe. I was not sure if I should engage him in conversation, but after a few silent moments of me just smiling sheepishly at him, I said, a little hesitantly, "I have come all the way from Kingston to see you." He smiled more broadly and said, "Do you know one Professor Michael Bucknor, who is the head of the English department at UWI in Jamaica?" I had to lean in close to him to hear him clearly. Then I said, "I am he!" and he repeated the answer "I am he" with a smile.

To this day, I was not clear whether he had recognized me from the start and was having fun at my expense or that he associated Kingston with me. Then he started to move his fingers on the flat control board for the television as if he were typing and I thought even here in this state, all he wanted to do was type—all he wanted to do was write.

On his last visit to Kingston, in early 2002, I was designated to host Austin, who had been specially invited as visiting writer to the Mona Campus. He conducted writing workshops, had a reading, visited my class "West Indian Special Author Seminar: Austin Clarke," donated parts of the manuscript of *The Polished Hoe* to me and to the UWI Library, and did an interview for the campus radio. In that interview he reported that the first time his Jamaican wife "cussed" some good Jamaican "bad words" to him was when he told her he wanted to take up writing as a full-time career. And since he made that decision sometime in the late 1950s/early 1960s, he continued to write and publish for a half a century. At the age eighty, he published his most recent memoir, *'Membering*, which was longlisted for the OCM Bocas and the RBC Taylor Prizes. From *The Survivors of the Crossing* in 1964 to *'Membering* in 2015, Clarke was writing and publishing for over fifty years. This in itself is a milestone—this longevity indicates his dedication to his craft and his commitment to archiving the lives of Black Barbadians, Caribbean-Canadians and African- and Caribbean-Americans.

On June 26, 2016 I arrived in London, where I was scheduled to give a paper on Clarke, only to receive news of his passing. That day I reflected on my earliest encounters with Clarke. I was an MPhil student at UWI Mona in 1991–92 and attending my first conference, which was the 1992 West Indian Literature Conference in Guyana. Like Pat Saunders, who spoke from the floor of the 2016 West Indian Literature Conference in Montego Bay, Jamaica, about the way in which the West Indian Literature Conference influenced her professional life, there is a story here about how this 1992 conference eventually directed my scholarly life. I was due to leave Jamaica for Canada that summer and heard a paper on "Exile in West Indian Literature" that featured Austin Clarke. I realized that some of the issues being discussed in that paper I might be facing soon, and my interest was piqued.

That summer, I met Clarke when I was co-opted into helping with the Association of Commonwealth Literature and Language Studies conference in Jamaica. I met him again at the University of Western Ontario, where I organized a reading series dubbed "Other Voices" for the Black Students Association; we invited Austin Clarke to be a presenter and from there a friendship developed.

My last special time with him was in 2011, when I visited Toronto and interviewed him in two four-hour marathon sessions over two days. His body was shaky; he was shuffling as he walked (and I was amazed at how age had altered this athlete, this "running fool" from Barbados, as he described himself in *Growing Up Stupid Under the Union Jack*). Yet, his mind was so sharp and his memory was so strong and he was still so excited about new writing projects. He gave me a copy of *More* that had just come out after over forty years of trying to place it and shared with me his first collection of poems, *Where the Sun Shines Best*, and showing me the scene before his house where a homeless man was killed—this homicide, the inspiration for the collection. He was generous and accommodating, in good humour and delightful company. When he became tired, I roamed through his ceiling-high bookcases in his house full of books.

Clarke was no doubt a complicated and sometimes controversial figure, but his commanding corpus of writings that is rich with inventive Barbadian dialect and that documented the lives of the Black Diaspora from Barbados, Canada, and America is a true legacy for Caribbean literature. In addition, his institution-building role for the reception of non-white Canadian writers in Canada, his racial activism, his pioneering work on Black studies programs in the American academy, his role as a diplomat, his media work in both Canada and Barbados, and his enthusiastic support of young writers have made him a significant Caribbean writer of our times. The unforgettable image of his fingers on an imaginary typewriter that day in May 2016 will remain a lasting memory for me of the man. All he wanted to do was write. May his soul rest in peace.

CHAPTER 30

Recognition

David Chariandy

I met him for the first time at an academic function, a downtown bar of the vaguely hip sort preferred by graduate students and faculty: local beer, alternative music, standing circles of subdued professional conversation. And when Rinaldo walked him into our midst, I wondered how this would play out. Here was Austin Clarke himself, debonair in his sports jacket and the bright tongue of a pocket square. I was wearing a black T-shirt earnestly tight; and when Rinaldo privately introduced me to the author, I got a nod but also a subtle look of disapproval. Austin afterwards made little effort to engage with me or any of the other "academicians" in our small group. One was doing most of the talking: about teaching, about theory, about celebrated new books. Austin remained quiet, pointedly so, until the talker deigned to address the newcomer. "I'm sorry," the talker began, "I don't believe I know who you are." "And why not?" Austin replied.

There was a lot of Austin in that reply, a lot of his insistent pride, and a lot, too, about the long and entirely unconcluded struggle faced by a generation of Black writers in securing due recognition in Canada, even among literary experts. When I met him in that bar, Austin was in fact no stranger to the academy. He had taught at Yale and Duke and had contributed in multiple ways to Black and Caribbean studies throughout the world. He was of course the author of many important and pivotal books, including *The Meeting Point*, the first novel to substantially evoke Black life in Canada. *The Meeting Point* focuses on a circle of Black domestic workers who, in the fifties and early sixties, were able to bypass Canadian immigration restrictions against people from the non-white world through the "West Indian Domestic Scheme." At one point in the novel, a worker named Bernice witnesses a protest on the Toronto streets against racial intolerance, but tells her friend Dots, "[T]hese niggers in Canada! Well, they don't know how lucky they are!" (305). Bernice continues to explain to Dots, also a domestic worker, that "this is Canada, dear, *not* America. You and me, we is West Indians, not American Negroes. We are not in that mess" (306). However, at the end of the novel, Bernice witnesses the brutal beating of a Black friend by police, experiencing the scene as "too real; and too much of a dream at the same time. The brutality and the violence" (341). And when Dots eventually sees this same friend in hospital, she exclaims, "I never knew that this place was so blasted cruel" (346).

I'd say that *The Meeting Point* stages a "recognition" markedly different from the "politics of recognition" as imagined by the philosopher Charles Taylor, wherein minorities appeal for judiciously measured attention from the state through institutionally legible enunciations of identity. But my first meeting with Austin presses me to focus on a separate if related matter—how certain writers, evoking certain issues in certain ways, can so easily go unrecognized. For me, the most striking cases here are of Black women like M. NourbeSe Philip, who in her own words risked being "disappeared"; or else the even more extreme case of Claire Harris, who did quite literally seem to vanish from Canadian letters, and whose poetic legacy is in need of due appreciation and custodianship. But I'm also now thinking of Sam Selvon, that indisputable giant of Caribbean literature and "nation language" for whom Austin wrote a book-long tribute, but whom, after moving to Canada and writing several books, was completely ignored, receiving not a single review here. For a while, Selvon supported himself by working as a janitor at the University of Calgary—an adequate symbol, one suspects, of the enduring relationship of the First World academy to the labour, cultural and otherwise, of the global South. The struggle for true recognition continues today among a new generation of Black and BIPOC writers who have found astonishingly innovative ways to write and share their works, but who must also confront unparalleled contractions and crises in traditional publishing, as well as steadily declining funding, institutional support, and venues for the informed discussion of their work. There remains the old problem of those who dismiss all writing they either naively or cynically deem "political." But newly amplified, today, is the problem of those with belated, voyeuristic, and ultimately passing curiosity in "the political" who refuse to treat Black writers as complex and disciplined artists and intellectuals.

But I think that in my first meeting with Austin in that bar there was a whole different sort of recognition, if that's how to describe it. For what word do we use to describe those forms of connection and intimacy that occur in Black life and potentially also among people of companion experiences and sensibilities— those experiences and calculations carried in gesture and voice, "in words and not in words," at turns covertly signalled and boldly declared? I don't know when exactly it was that I told Austin that my own mother had been of that generation of Black domestic workers he decided to write about. I know it wasn't upon our first meeting at that bar, in that particular air of knowing and ignorance. But it was nevertheless in that moment when Austin and I began connecting, my tight T-shirt notwithstanding. He did, most certainly, support my work, but here, too, there is something to tell. Despite his best efforts at the very height of his career, Austin simply couldn't convince the mainstream literary establishment of whatever potential he saw in me. And it was in fact through the collective effort of younger and less "connected" authors like Wayde Compton, Ashok Mathur, and Larissa Lai, as well as Brian Lam and Robert Ballantyne of the fiercely independent Arsenal Pulp Press, that my first book was eventually published. Austin's gift to me was not a door to "the establishment" or "literary celeb-rity" swung widely open, for he himself had limited access to these things. Instead, he offered me things infinitely more meaning-ful—writerly friendship and a living link with a powerful tradition.

Austin Clarke.
Permissions: William Ready Division of Archives and Research Collections, McMaster University Library

In his last years, Austin would often ask about the next novel I was writing, the one he hoped would experience the "sophomore" success he himself never enjoyed. He never lived to see this novel published; and when I dedicated it to him posthumously, I understood the gesture to be at once sincere and complex. A poet I know—a man, I'd point out—once insisted that dedications or mottos are never homages ordinarily imagined, but rather something like a declaration of war. And I get that to some extent. Stylistically, Austin and I were very different, both in dress and also on the page. We were Black men with Caribbean roots; but his were Bajan and mine were what he wryly called "Trickidadian." Austin showed me love, but he sometimes expressed impatience with my doubts and moments of quiet —"Stop acting like the young men in your books," he once complained. He was at one point reputed to be "the angriest Black man in Canada," but his cultural politics were often as challenging to parse as some of his most gorgeously baroque sentences, being either brilliantly anarchic or else outright contradictory: socialist in one breath and candidate for the Progressive Conservative Party in another. And behind it all were our generational differences: the fact that he was "the immigrant" of that postwar group of Caribbean émigrés who sought possibility here, but who learned in new terms their Blackness; and the fact that I was of the rising numbers of the "the born here," narrated lifelong by the nation of our birth as unwanted outsiders, but knowing intimately no other space, and needing some imaginative alternative, some greater story of being. Yet this generational difference seemed to connect Austin and I the strongest. In the novels we each wrote during the years of our friendship, I kept imagining that we were reaching out to each other. His Bernice and Dots echoing my Adele and Ruth. His BJ the family of my Michael and Francis. Austin taught me that kinship is never a sameness but a loving seeing across distance.

I don't recall Austin and I ever again attending another academic function. When we met, it was in bars of his choosing—noisy, upscale places of wealth and transit where upon entering you would quickly spot him. And I most often remember seating myself slightly apart from the man, sometimes across a table, or most often on adjacent angles of a cornered bar—"on the diagonal," as Dionne Brand once put it—which always seemed Austin's favorite way to sit and drink, and perhaps his chosen way to live. Rinaldo was always with us, for he remained until the end Austin's closest confidant, the most intimate sharer of his jokes and tales and brilliance, and Abdi was there too, and in the best moments Dionne and Leslie. In his last months of declining health, Austin abandoned jackets for more comfortable clothes, but he was always stylish, his dreads magnificent. I still see him like that, speaking his magic, or else quiet and regal in the din of conversation about us. He's working on his third martini, and when our eyes meet he smiles and lifts his glass.

Works Cited

Algoo-Baksh, Stella. *Austin C. Clarke: A Biography*. ECW Press, 1994.

Barrett, Paul. "'Our Words Spoken among Us, in Fragments': Austin Clarke's Aesthetics of Crossing." *Journal of West Indian Literature*, vol. 23, nos. 1–2, 2015, pp. 89–105.

Beattie, Steven. W. Rev. *In Your Crib* by Austin Clarke. *Quill and Quire*, vol. 81, no. 3, 2015, p. 33.

Benjamin, Walter. "Unpacking My Library." *Illuminations*, edited by Hannah Arendt; translated by Harry Zohn, Schocken Books, 1968, pp. 59–68.

Bhabha, Homi. "Unpacking My Library Again." *Journal of the Midwest Modern Language Association*, vol. 28, no. 1, 1995, pp. 5–18.

Brand, Dionne. *A Map to the Door of No Return: Notes to Belonging*. Random House, 2001.

———. *thirsty*. McClelland and Stewart, 2002.

Bucknor, Michael A. "'Voices Under the Window' of Representation: Austin Clarke's Poetics of (Body) Memory in *The Meeting Point*." *Journal of West Indian Literature*, vol. 13, nos. 1–2, 2005, pp. 141–75.

Clarke, Austin. *Amongst Thistles and Thorns*. McClelland and Stewart, 1966.

———. "Bonanza 1972 in Toronto." *Choosing His Coffin: The Best Short Stories of Austin Clarke*, edited by Patrick Crean and Sarah Williams, Thomas Allen, 2003, pp. 261–76.

———. "Canadian Experience." *Choosing His Coffin: The Best Short Stories of Austin Clarke*, Thomas Allen, 2003, pp. 23–39.

———. "The Discipline." *Choosing His Coffin: The Best Short Stories of Austin Clarke*, Thomas Allen, 2003, pp. 1–21.

———. "Fishermen Looking Out to Sea." *The Austin Clarke Reader*, edited by Barry Callaghan, Exile Editions, 1996, pp. 253–55.

———. "Five Poems from Barbados." *The Review* [Trinity College, University of Toronto], vol. 69, no. 3, 1957, pp. 23–25.

———. "From My Lover's Home." *The Austin Clarke Reader*, edited by Barry Callaghan, Exile Editions, 1996, p. 254.

———. *Growing Up Stupid Under the Union Jack.* 1980. McClelland and Stewart, 2005.

———. "He Walks Beside the Sea." *The Review* [Trinity College, University of Toronto], vol. 69, no. 4, 1957, p. 33.

———. "Her Hair Is Plaited Tight." *Callaloo,* vol. 37, no. 1, 2014, pp. 36–52.

———. "In my barefoot days, under the sun, blackened." *Evidence,* vol. 1, 1960, n.p.

———. *In This City.* Exile Editions, 1992.

———. *In Your Crib.* Guernica Editions, 2015.

———. "Kirkland, North by North." *Evidence,* vol. 2, 1961, n.p.

———. *The Meeting Point.* MacMillan, 1967.

———. *'Membering.* Dundurn, 2015.

———. *More.* Thomas Allen, 2008.

———. "The Motor Car." *When He Was Free and Young and He Used to the Wear Silks,* House of Anansi, 1971, pp. 90–111.

———. *Nine Men Who Laughed.* Penguin, 1986.

———. *A Passage Back Home: A Personal Reminiscence of Sam Selvon.* Exile Editions, 1994.

———. *Pig Tails 'n Breadfruit: Rituals of Slave Food.* Ian Randle, 1999.

———. *The Polished Hoe.* Thomas Allen, 2003.

———. "Public Enemies: Police Violence and Black Youth." *The Austin Clarke Reader,* edited by Barry Callaghan, Exile Editions, 1996, pp. 324–44.

———. "The Rogue in Me." *The Review* [Trinity College, University of Toronto], vol. 69, no. 4, 1957, p. 13.

———. "A Short Drive." *Choosing His Coffin: The Best Short Stories of Austin Clarke,* Thomas Allen, 2003, pp. 79–98.

———. *The Survivors of the Crossing.* McClelland and Stewart, 1964.

———. "They Heard a Ringing of the Bells." *When He Was Free and Young and He Used To Wear Silks,* House of Anansi, 1971, pp. 16–29.

———. "They're Not Coming Back." *Choosing His Coffin: The Best Stories of Austin Clarke,* Thomas Allen, 2003, pp. 163–79.

———. "Waiting for the Postman to Knock." *When He Was Free and Young and He Used to Wear Silks,* House of Anansi, 1971, pp. 30–50.

———. "The West Indian Immigrant in Canada." William Ready Archives, McMaster University, Box 20, Folder 14.

———. "When He was Free and Young and He Used to Wear Silks" *When He Was Free and Young and Used to Wear Silks*, House of Anansi, 1971, pp. 140–51.

———. *Where the Sun Shines Best.* Guernica Editions, 2013.

———. "Why I Call Johnson Killing Murderous." *Contrast* [Toronto], Aug. 30, 1979, p. 12.

Clyne, Kalifa. "T&T Food Crisis Looming." *Trinidad and Tobago Guardian*, Mar. 19, 2016.

Coleman, Daniel. *Masculine Migrations.* U of Toronto P, 1998.

Fanon, Frantz. *Black Skin, White Masks.* Translated by Charles Lam Markmann, Grove Press, 1952.

Gilmore, David D. *Misogyny: The Male Malady.* U of Pennsylvania P, 2001.

Grainger, James. Rev. *More* by Austin Clarke. *Quill and Quire*, Sept. 22, 2008, https://quillandquire.com/review/more/.

Gray, Charlotte. "Carol." *Ottawa Citizen*, July 20, 2003.

Hawthorne, Nathaniel. *The Scarlet Letter.* Doubleday, 1898.

Isaacs, Camille A. "Still Angry: An Interview with Austin Clarke." *Austin Clarke: Essays on His Works*, edited by Camille A. Isaacs, Guernica Editions, 2013, pp. 13–27.

Johnson, W. Chris. "Guerrilla Ganja Gun Girls: Policing Black Revolutionaries from Notting Hill to Laventille." *Gender, Imperialism and Global Exchanges*, edited by Stephan F. Miescher et al., Wiley Blackwell, 2015, pp. 280–306.

Marshall, Paule. "From the Poets in the Kitchen." *Reena and Other Stories*, The Feminist Press, 1983.

———. "To Da-Duh, in Memoriam." *Reena and Other Stories*, The Feminist Press, 1983.

———. *Triangular Road: A Memoir.* Civitas Books, 2009.

McAloon, Jonathan. "Can Male Writers Avoid Misogyny?" *The Guardian* [London], May 4, 2017, https://www.theguardian.com/books/booksblog/2017/may/04/can-male-writers-avoid-misogyny.

Mehta, Brinda. "The Mother as Culinary Griotte: Food and Cultural Memory in Austin Clarke's *Pig Tails 'n Breadfruit.*" *Austin Clarke:*

Essays on His Works, edited by Camille A. Isaacs, Guernica Editions, 2013, pp. 323–64.

Morrison, Toni. *Beloved*. Knopf, 1987.

———. *Playing in the Dark: Whiteness and the Literary Imagination*. Harvard UP, 1992.

———. "The Site of Memory." *What Moves at the Margins: Selected Nonfiction*, edited by Carolyn C. Denard, UP of Mississippi, 2008, pp. 65–81.

Mount, Nick. *Arrival: The Story of CanLit*. House of Anansi, 2017.

National Post. "Austin Clarke, 'Canada's First Multicultural Writer' and Giller Prize–Winning Author, Dead at 81." *National Post* [Toronto], June 26, 2016, https://nationalpost.com/entertainment/books/ austin-clarke-canadas-first-multicultural-writer-and-giller-prize -winning-author-dead-at-81#.

Pound, Ezra. *The Cantos of Ezra Pound*. Faber, 1975.

Quirt, Maggie. "'A Plea of Love and Blood': Social Justice in Austin Clarke's *Where the Sun Shines Best*." *Austin Clarke: Essays on His Works*, edited by Camille A. Isaacs, Guernica Editions, 2013, pp. 387–91.

Renan, Ernest. *What Is a Nation? And Other Political Writings*. Columbia UP, 2018.

Sanders, Leslie. "Austin Clarke's Poetic Turn." *Confluences 1: Essays on the New Canadian Literature*, edited by Nurjehan Aziz, Mawenzi House, 2016, pp. 65–75.

Saunders, Patricia J. "Fugitive Dreams of Diaspora: Conversations with Saidiya Hartman." *Anthurium: A Caribbean Studies Journal*, vol. 6, no. 1, 2008, p. 7.

Sharpe, Christina. *In the Wake: On Blackness and Being*. Duke UP, 2016.

———. *Monstrous Intimacies: Making Post-Slavery Subjects*. Duke UP, 2010.

Singh, Kris. "Archived Relationships: Pierre Bourdieu and Writers of the Caribbean Diaspora." *Bourdieu and Postcolonial Studies*, edited by Raphael Dalleo, Liverpool UP, 2016, pp. 175–90.

Smith, Arthur James Marshall. "Eclectic Detachment: Aspects of Identity in Canadian Poetry." *Canadian Literature*, vol. 9, 1961, pp. 6–14.

Spillers, Hortense J. "Mama's Baby, Papa's Maybe: An American Grammar Book." *Diacritics*, vol. 17, no. 2, 1987, pp. 64–81.

Springer, Jennifer Thorington. "Constructing Radical Black Female Subjectivities: Survival Pimping in Austin Clarke's *The Polished Hoe.*" *Frontiers: A Journal of Women Studies*, vol. 36, no. 2, 2015, pp. 169–91. *Project MUSE*, muse.jhu.edu/article/589419.

Turco, Lewis. *The Book of Forms.* Dutton, 1968.

Waters, Rob. *Thinking Black: Britain, 1964–1985.* U of California P, 2019.

Wentzell, Emily A. *Maturing Masculinities: Aging, Chronic Illness, and Viagra in Mexico.* Duke UP, 2013.

Index